STONEWALL INN EDITIONS
Keith Kahla, General Editor

ALSO BY BRIAN MCNAUGHT
On Being Gay

GAY ISSUES
IN THE
WORKPLACE

Brian McNaught

St. Martin's Press / New York

Design by Sara Stemen

Library of Congress Cataloging-in-Publication Data

McNaught, Brian.
Gay issues in the workplace / Brian McNaught.—Stonewall Inn ed.
p. cm.
Includes bibliographical references.
ISBN 0-312-11798-1
1. Gays—Employment—United States. 2. Homosexuality—United
States. I. Title.
HD6285.5.U6M38 1995
331.5—dc20 94-36063 CIP

First Paperback Edition: January 1995
10 9 8 7 6 5 4 3 2 1

This book is dedicated to Mary Lee Tatum, my dear friend and colleague who co-facilitated the "Homophobia in the Workplace" workshop for the first three years. Mary Lee was a pioneer and visionary in the field of sexuality education. Her warmth, generosity, and spirit, combined with her enormous skills as an educator, made her a delight to work with and a highlight of the workshop. When she died in an automobile accident on June 1, 1991, I lost one of my best friends, the field of sexuality education lost a real hero, and the world lost one of its nicest family members.

Contents

Acknowledgments

THIS BOOK REFLECTS the generous, thoughtful input from a special group of family members, colleagues, and friends. Each person brought to the reading of this manuscript unique insights and skills that clarified and strengthened the text.

Thank you Ray Struble, my partner in life; my father, Waldo McNaught; Joan McNaught, my aunt; my brother, Tom McNaught; and David Struble, also my brother. Beyond your reputation and expertise as successful corporate executives, AIDS/communications specialist, and human resource manager, your enthusiasm for this project was very important to me.

Colleagues and friends who read and worked with me on this book are Art Bain, Claire Brown, Jerry Dark, Michael Denneny (my editor at St. Martin's Press), Kathleen Dermody, David Dotlich, Doug Elwood, Ariadne Kane, Mark Kaplan, Rhona Lava, Jay Lucas, Steve Mershon, Ed Mickens, Bianca Cody Murphy, Wayne Pawlowski, Karen Siebert, Bill Stayton, Cooper Thompson, and John Ware (my agent). In that group, there are some of the nation's top sexuality educators, trainers, human resource experts, and authorities on gay issues in the workplace. There is also a person or two who rightfully should be listed among my family. Thank you all for your enthusiastic and timely response to my request for help.

Finally, I thank one special woman who also falls into all three categories of family, colleague, and friend: Pam Wilson, my co-facilitator in the "Homophobia in the Workplace" workshop, provided me with constant editorial assistance. Her hard work and thoughtful, expert advice kept me believing this book would not only be completed, but that it would be a valuable contribution to the discussion of gay issues in the workplace.

Introduction

Unprecedented numbers of gay, lesbian, and bisexual people today are publicly acknowledging who they are and what they need from their employers to be fully productive members of the workplace. This book offers guidance in understanding and responding to the important business concern of gay issues in the workplace.

Employers want to know:

"Why are gay people 'coming out' (identifying their sexual orientation) at work, and what do they want?"

"Why do corporations need to address this issue, and how can they do so effectively?"

"How do we talk with heterosexual co-workers and customers about this issue in a way that will make allies of them?"

Understanding and addressing the issues raised by gay, lesbian, and bisexual employees requires a commitment like that made by corporations to understand and address the needs of African Americans, Latinos, women, Jews, the disabled, and others who face obstacles in their efforts to be fully productive members of the workplace. The process begins with an awareness there is a problem

In the "Homophobia in the Workplace" training sessions I have been doing in corporations for the last several years, my colleagues and I help employees better understand the problem. We begin by leading the workshop participants in an exercise that asks them to assess the climate for gay people in their workplace and how they feel about being with gay people. After deciding whether the atmosphere for gay employees is "very hostile," "somewhat hostile," "somewhat accepting," or "very accepting," the group then decides whether they think it best that their gay co-workers "stay in the closet," "come out only to a few close friends," "come out to their supervisors," or "come out to everyone." Once these decisions have been made, the workshop participants are invited to an imaginary company picnic.

"Let's pretend that everyone wants to come to this company picnic and all are invited to bring significant others and children, if they have them," we say. "Would you be most comfortable if your gay, lesbian, and bisexual co-workers would 'come with a date of the other sex,' 'come alone,' 'come with a same-sex date but refrain from showing any signs of affection,' or 'come with a same-sex date and feel as comfortable as heterosexual co-workers do in showing signs of affection'?" *Signs of affection* is defined as the kind of behavior that couples engage in publicly to indicate that they are a couple. Hand holding is offered as an example.

The responses of the several thousand American corporate personnel who have been through this workshop offer us a perspective on the multiple issues involved in the discussion of gay people in the workplace. Curiously, in answer to the first question—"How would you describe the atmosphere for gay, lesbian, and bisexual employees in your workplace?"—most employees believe the workplace is "somewhat accepting" for gay people. The same majority says, however, they would recommend that a gay co-worker "stay in the closet" or "come out only to a few close friends," even when the company has a non-discrimination policy that includes sexual orientation.

In response to question three, a handful of people say gay colleagues should come to the office picnic alone. More than half of the participants say they would be most comfortable if gay co-workers "come with a same-sex partner but refrain from displaying any signs of affection." The remaining people say "come . . . and feel as comfortable as heterosexual co-workers do in showing signs of affection."

We then ask, "What really happens? What choice do you think your gay co-workers make? Do they bring same-sex dates to company social functions?"

"They stay home or come alone" is the usual reply.

Then my colleagues and I are asked a question. In each session, someone will say:

"Why does someone have to tell us he or she is gay?"

That is an important and timely question. Gay men and lesbian women, estimated by researchers to make up between one and 10 percent of the work force in the United States,[1] are coming out in seemingly every profession. Gay caucuses or support groups have been formed for attorneys, engineers, social workers, reporters, doctors, clergy, police officers, book publishers, teachers, and politicians, to name only a few. The question for many heterosexual co-workers is "Why?" More to the point, the question is often posed, "I don't tell people what I do in bed. Why must they tell us what they do in bed?"

Being gay, from this perspective, is understood in only sexual terms. The question, I feel, generally isn't hostile. More often than not it reflects confusion and some fear, based upon a lack of information and understanding. That lack of understanding often manifests itself into a problem in the workplace.

Many companies today recognize there is a problem and are working to address it. A large and ever-increasing number of American businesses, for instance, have added the words *sexual orientation* to their non-discrimination policies. Several corporations, like those for which I work (AT&T and Bell Communications Research), attempting to acknowledge and capitalize upon the diversity of today's work force, are offering training for their management and employees on the issues faced by gay, lesbian, and bisexual co-workers. Some companies such as Lotus, Levi Strauss, and MCA, as well as municipalities like Boston, Seattle, and West Hollywood, offer an assortment of benefits to the "domestic partners" of their gay workers. Some airlines have amended frequent-flier rules to recognize unmarried partners. Some department stores are extending discounts to the domestic partners of their unmarried employees, and some colleges are changing housing regulations that formerly prohibited unmarried graduate students and faculty from living in university facilities with partners of their choice.

For many people, without benefit of explanation, these developments may make no sense. Such efforts to offer equitable treatment to gay people can appear to be "just more affirmative-action silliness" or "an erosion of the American family ethic." The emergence of gay people in the work force can be perplexing morally, personally, and professionally to some heterosexual co-workers. The confusion can be compounded when the heterosexual is from another culture in which there is little or no discussion of homosexuality, or when the heterosexual belongs to a religious group that rigorously opposes homosexual behavior.

Questions commonly heard from my workshop participants are:

"Will acknowledging the presence of gay co-workers mean to others that I approve of homosexuality?"

"If I went to a company picnic with my children and they saw a gay couple holding hands, would it influence my children's development?"

"If I refuse to share an office with a gay person, will I be fired?"

"Does this mean companies are going to have a gay quota in hiring?"

"Gay people choose to be gay, don't they? How, then, can you compare gay issues to those issues faced by people of color and women?"

The management of corporations and other organizations wrestling with the emergence of gay people in the workplace likewise have lots of questions. They include:

"The federal government doesn't require us to protect gay employees from discrimination, so why should we?"

"How do we make sure that we don't come across as endorsing a lifestyle?"

"What's this going to cost? Can we afford to pay for domestic-partner benefits?"

"Would it be discrimination not to send an openly gay person to represent us with a client who disapproves of homosexuality?"

"What do we do with our employees who have strong negative feelings about homosexuality?"

"Will there be a public backlash?"

"If we address the needs of this group, who's next in line—transvestites?"

The questions that surround this issue, I propose, are not all that different than the questions raised in the past or even today on other diversity issues confronting an employer. Such questions include:

"Am I discriminating against a person of color if I don't send him or her to represent us with a racist client?"

"How do I acknowledge holidays without endorsing a particular religion?"

"What if a Jew doesn't want to work with an Arab, or vice versa?"

"What do we do with employees who strongly object on moral or religious grounds to serving alcohol at company functions, or to divorce, or to interfaith marriage?"

As is true with other tough issues of diversity, the corporate incentive in recognizing the presence of gay people in the workplace is productivity. A mutually respectful work force that acknowledges and affirms its diversity is not only typically more productive, but also attracts and retains the "best and the brightest" employees. Likewise, I believe the solution to employee confusion and angst over the corporation addressing the needs of gay workers is the same as it has been to other areas of conflict—education. To that end, this book has been written.

I have addressed here a number of the many issues raised in discussions of gay people in the workplace. Based upon my experience as a trainer and educator, I offer:

1. premises for successfully framing the issue;
2. an understanding of who gay, lesbian, and bisexual people are, why they come out, and how they do so;
3. explanations of heterosexism and homophobia and of how they impact the workplace;
4. an exploration of what gay people want and need to feel safe, valued, and fully productive;
5. answers to commonly asked questions;
6. a model for training on this issue.

Much of the anecdotal information in this book comes from the workshop "Homophobia in the Workplace" I designed and have offered since 1988 as either a whole- or half-day training session. The primary audience has been telecommunications employees throughout the United States. The thousands of men and women who have attended the workshop to date represent a broad cross section by age, ethnic background, religious affiliation, geographical location, culture, educational level, and job description. There are almost always members of management in every workshop, with some sessions made up entirely of supervisors. Approximately half of the attendees are "strongly encouraged" to attend by their management. The others sign up out of interest or because they are satisfying a yearly requirement to attend at least one diversity workshop.

Sometimes a member of the class will identify him- or herself as a gay, lesbian, or bisexual person, but in the majority of groups no one does so. Often during a break, the parent, child, or sibling of a gay person will privately identify him- or herself. For many of them, it is the first time in the work environment they feel able to acknowledge they have a gay or lesbian relative.

The opinions expressed and information offered in this book are also based upon nearly twenty years of working as an educator of gay and lesbian issues. My audiences include students and university personnel, police officers, clergy and religious, coaches, health-care workers, parents, and social-service providers, among others. It likewise reflects my experiences as a gay man and the experiences of the hundreds of gay, lesbian, and bisexual people who have shared their insights with me.

Gay Issues
in the
Workplace

1 / Premises

I RECENTLY RECEIVED a promotional flier for a conference entitled "Invisible Diversity: A Gay and Lesbian Corporate Agenda." The conference, the first of its kind, was sponsored by a variety of gay* groups (N.Y. Gay and Lesbian Community Center, the Human Rights Campaign Fund), the Waldorf-Astoria, and the New York City Mayor's Office, with participation by Levi Strauss, U.S. West, Digital, Coors Brewing, and AT&T.

On the back of the flier, I was quoted. More accurately, I was *mis*quoted. In support of the workshop, I had offered the following statement:

"When gay and lesbian workers can't work safely, they can't work at optimum productivity. Eliminating homophobia from the workplace profits everyone. Educational efforts such as this are critically important first steps."

The program, however, had me saying, "Eliminating *hysteria* from the workplace profits everyone."

When I called the man to whom I had given the quote, he responded to my complaint by saying, "It was a printer's error." He then offered, "Besides, some of the responses we've received to our flier *have* been hysterical. We've had death threats!"

Responding to an invitation to attend a conference on gay

---

* See note on language at the end of this chapter.

issues in the workplace with a death threat is a hysterical response, and there are times when gay employees in corporate America receive death threats. The increased visibility of gay people in society and in the workplace has brought into the open some people's fear and hatred of homosexuality (also known as *homophobia*). Gay, lesbian, and bisexual employees in one of the corporations in which I work, for instance, have been threatened by name through bathroom graffiti and telephone calls and mail to their office and home. Clearly, such a hysterical response to the presence of gay people in the workplace is ignorant, as well as outrageous, counterproductive, and criminal.

But even if we found and educated—or fired—the handful of people who make such hysterical threats, gay, lesbian, and bisexual people in the workplace would still encounter regular expressions of homophobia. Rather than a death threat, it is much more likely gay workers today will hear a gay joke, the inappropriate use of language, such as a "fag" or "dyke" comment, or an AIDS joke. They are also likely to see an anti-gay cartoon or article taped to an office file cabinet or door. And if it's not a homophobic comment, it is often a heterosexist remark or question that creates anxiety, anger, frustration, or distraction. (Heterosexism is the belief that everyone is heterosexual or ought to be.) Gay people who are presumed to be heterosexual are told gay and AIDS jokes, are offered to be set up on dates and are asked whom they are dating, why they are not dating, whom they will bring to the office party or holiday dance, or how and with whom they are spending or have spent their weekend or holiday.

It should go without saying that death threats take a toll on an employee's ability to produce at his or her highest level. I believe, as do an ever-increasing number of corporations, universities, and municipalities, that the jokes, comments, and heterosexist assumptions also take a heavy toll and prevent the gay, lesbian, and bisexual employee, and those who care about them, from putting all of their energies into their job. In other words, homophobia is bad for business. It affects productivity.

Before making a stronger case for how homophobia affects everyone in the workplace, I offer for consideration the following assumptions:

GAY PEOPLE ARE PRESENT IN THE WORKPLACE

I assume that there are gay, lesbian, and bisexual people in every profession in every area of the world. While cultural attitudes prevent most of these people from acknowledging their orientation or prevent them from behaving sexually in a way that is consistent with their orientation, homosexual people have lived, live now, and will continue to live in every age, culture, race, religion, gender, economic level, and profession.

No one knows for sure how many gay people there are in the world. For many years, social scientists relied upon Alfred Kinsey's groundbreaking research on American sexual behavior. Published in 1948 and in 1953, the Kinsey studies said that in a sample of nearly 12,000 men and women, approximately 10 percent of the respondents were either exclusively homosexual or predominantly homosexual in their behavior.[1] Based upon that figure, most sexuality professionals reasoned that at least 10 percent of the population was therefore homosexual in their internal feelings of attraction.

Other studies have both supported and challenged Kinsey's findings. The recently released Janus Report, for instance, estimates that 9 percent of American men are homosexual and 5 percent of women.[2] On the other hand, the Alan Guttmacher Institute created considerable public debate with its study that found only 1 percent of male respondents acknowledged being gay. Of the 3,321 men in their twenties and thirties who were questioned in that survey, only 2.3 percent reported having had any same-sex sexual experience.[3]

In this book, I make important distinctions between *sexual orientation, sexual behavior,* and *sexual identity.* It is quite possible that 10 or more percent of the population is homosexual in orientation, 3 to 5 percent is homosexual in behavior, and only 1 to 2 percent is homosexual in identity. Given current cultural attitudes toward homosexuality, common sense encourages the belief that there would be such differences in numbers.

Insofar as I am addressing the need to create a safe and productive work environment, I don't think it makes much difference how many employees identify themselves as gay or how many employees have a homosexual orientation, any more than it matters how many employees are directly affected by anti-Semitism.

For our purposes, I will continue to use 10 percent as an estimate of the numbers of people who have a homosexual orientation. It is the figure with which I am most familiar and comfortable. Using that estimate for the general population, it follows, then, that up to 10 percent of the work force is gay or lesbian. The number is probably higher in some professions and lower in others, but in most of the corporate world I assume it is about 10 percent.

In addition to those whom we would classify as homosexual, there is an even larger percentage of people who are bisexual in their orientation. Kinsey reported that 37 percent of the men interviewed reported a same-sex experience that led to orgasm, and 13 percent of the women reported same-sex behavior. The Janus study said 22 percent of their male respondents and 17 percent of their female respondents had same-sex experiences. Bisexual people are men and women who have erotic/romantic feelings for or attractions to both sexes. Sometimes those attractions have equal intensity, and sometimes a bisexual person is more attracted to one gender than the other. Regardless, bisexual people often experience the same oppression with regard to homophobic and heterosexist comments and behaviors.

Add to these numbers the parents and brothers and sisters of gay people who work in the corporate world. Add the children, aunts and uncles, grandparents, and friends of gay, lesbian, and bisexual people, and the percentage of workers affected by homophobia becomes staggering. And add to these numbers those individuals who have intensely negative feelings about homosexuality and we find that this topic can affect the vast majority of the work force. If you aren't gay, aren't related to or a friend to a gay person, aren't anti-gay, you more than likely work next to and with someone who is.

HOMOPHOBIA EXISTS IN THE WORKPLACE

I propose, too, that homophobia exists everywhere. Homophobia is the fear and hatred of homosexuality in ourselves and in others. I know that even today it's a new word for some people. The U.S. Census Bureau called me because they were confused by how I identified my profession. "It says here you are a homophobia educator," they said.

"That's right," I replied.

"Well, we don't know what that is, but we think it's for people who are afraid of leaving the house. Are we right?"

I once was asked by a university official, "How do you know if the environment is homophobic?" I responded, "Presume it is." I said this because homophobia and heterosexism permeate our culture. Homophobic behavior is perhaps more expected in some specific professions, ethnic and religious groups, from some age, education, and economic levels, in some regions of the country more than others, but experience tells me that homophobia exists everywhere.

Sometimes homophobia is blatant. The week before I was scheduled to speak at the University of Vermont, a young man was kicked into a coma in an alley outside of a gay bar by a man who told police he had searched for a homosexual to beat up. That's homophobia. At one corporation with which I work, an employee put a sign on the office door that read: "Help stomp out AIDS. Kill a queer." That too is homophobia.

I met a man at that same corporation whose son had died of AIDS. A lot of people in the corporate world know someone who is HIV-positive, has AIDS, or has died from the disease. AIDS jokes and anti-gay comments can make these people angry and upset. When that happens, they think about what they wish they had said or done in response to the joke but didn't. They sit at their desks and fume. They may pick up the phone and call their friend with AIDS. They don't want to work with the co-worker who told the joke or made the comment. It has affected their attitude about the workplace and their productivity. Like homophobia, AIDSphobia—the fear and hatred of AIDS, of people infected with HIV, and of people suspected to be at risk of HIV infection—is bad for business.

Despite the facts that throughout the world, 75 percent of those infected with HIV—the virus responsible for AIDS— are heterosexual, and that well over 90 percent of newly infected adults acquire their HIV-infections from heterosexual intercourse,[4] many uninformed people continue to associate AIDS with homosexuality. This misguided association has two highly destructive and dangerous results: It creates and adds to the unjustifiable fear of an entire group of people (homosexuals), and it fosters a reckless sense of security among those heterosexuals who do not see AIDS as a threat to them personally. Like homophobia, AIDSphobia stems from fear and misinformation and makes the workplace a difficult environment in which to perform one's job.

HOMOPHOBIA AFFECTS PRODUCTIVITY

Gay people who have to worry about what will happen to them if they come out of the closet (acknowledge their homosexuality), generally produce at a lower level than gay people who don't worry about what will happen to them. Even when the company has a policy that forbids discrimination based upon sexual orientation, as many do today, gay employees will probably be less productive if they are afraid of coming out because of the hostility they hear and see in the workplace.

It takes a lot of energy to protect your private life. On a day-to-day basis, the closeted gay person in the corporate world leaves behind who they are, what is important to them, and what motivates them to succeed. He or she puts on a mask. Keeping that mask on to avoid discrimination is hard work.

It is hard work to dodge questions about what you did for Thanksgiving and what your weekend plans are. It is difficult to refrain from participating in discussions about family and friends. It takes energy to keep from being honest about oneself.

Closeted gay employees do not put on their desk a picture of the person they care most about for fear of being asked, "Who's that?" Closeted gay, lesbian, or bisexual employees do not make or receive personal phone calls in front of their co-workers. Closeted gay employees do not attend office social functions unless they come alone and wear that suffocating mask.

Once when my partner, Ray, and I were vacationing at Disney World, he spotted a colleague. Not being "out" at the time, he did not know how to introduce me to this man, his wife, and their children. I wandered off in another direction before their chance encounter. We met up later when the co-worker was out of sight. I was angry and hurt. Ray was angry, hurt, and resentful. We had long moments of difficult silence.

That is not an uncommon scenario. Closeted gay, lesbian, or bisexual employees face work-related stress inside and outside the workplace. Not only must they keep their masks on at the office, but also, when in the company of gay friends or their significant others, at restaurants, movies, bowling alleys, supermarkets, or church. If they are afraid of coming out of the closet at work, they will probably also be afraid of writing a letter to the editor about a gay issue; of marching in a gay parade; of any behavior that might be seen by someone who knows someone who works with them.

A friend of mine called to say she loved my book, *On Being Gay*. This friend, a lesbian woman who owns her own business, said she read my book on an airplane.

I asked her, "How did the people around you react?"

"Oh," she said, "I ripped the cover off."

Are there any books that a heterosexual person might so fear reading in public that he or she would rip off the cover? For closeted gay, lesbian, and bisexual people there are. And if this is true for a closeted woman who owns her own business, what would be the level of fear for closeted workers who depend upon compatibility with co-workers for their livelihood?

It is homophobia in the workplace that tells me I am not safe, that I must keep on the mask. It is homophobia that distracts me from my work either as a gay person who hears anti-gay comments at the lunchroom table or as the parent of a gay child with AIDS who walks by a sign about "killing queers" on the way to my office.

Many corporations today are saying, "We don't want our gay workers to be so afraid, so distracted, so angry. We don't want their productivity or that of the family and friends of gay people to be affected. How can we change things?" The answer, I believe, is through education. Homophobia is a fear and a hatred based upon ignorance. Education alleviates ignorance. But does it work for everybody?

I am often asked whether it is harder to work with blue-collar workers more than it is white-collar, with men more than women, with Southerners more than Northerners, with Catholics more than Unitarians. I have worked throughout the country with all ages and all types—with coaches and athletes, police officers and offenders, college students and high school dropouts, corporate executives and factory workers, clergy and agnostics, doctors and people with AIDS—and have found that people are people. Sometimes a particular audience is initially less receptive than another, but the end result is almost always the same. Which brings me to my next premise.

IGNORANCE IS THE ENEMY

I believe that ignorance, or lack of familiarity, is the parent of fear. We are generally afraid of what we don't understand. And fear is the parent of hatred. Though some hatred is learned, we otherwise often hate what we are afraid of. Homophobia is most often caused by a lack of accurate information about and familiarity with gay people. I believe that the problem of homophobia in the workplace is most effectively addressed through education.

BEHAVIOR, NOT BELIEFS, IS THE ISSUE

One final premise for our consideration is that tolerance does not mean acceptance and that challenging homophobic behaviors in the workplace does not mean we have to change people's beliefs or values. While I do feel that the jokes that are told about gay people often result from ignorance about homosexuality and about how those comments affect gay co-workers, I also feel that people are entitled to believe whatever they want about homosexuality and, for that matter, anything else. Corporations today are not in the business of dictating personal beliefs about gender, race, religion, or sexual orientation. The policies that prohibit discrimination are guidelines for behavior, not thought.

In the workplace today, people have varying beliefs on any number of topics, from politics to religion. Many people think divorce and birth control are forbidden by the Bible, but most of them would acknowledge that those are their personal beliefs; they wouldn't suggest that those who are divorced or who practice birth control should be discriminated against or be the butt of humor. Likewise, there are people who believe that homosexual behavior is forbidden by the Bible. This too is a personal belief.

In the workshops I have conducted, I have had numerous conversations with people who privately identify themselves as fundamentalist Christians. Many of them have confessed to me that they didn't know much about homosexuality; they still believe it is wrong for a homosexual to act on his or her sexual feelings, but they agree that it is wrong to discriminate against a homosexual person in the workplace.

Tolerance does not mean acceptance. We can monitor inappropriate behaviors in the workplace and allow people to hold personal, private beliefs.

Given these premises, the challenge to the employer who seeks to create a work environment in which all employees, including those who are gay, lesbian, and bisexual, can grow to their full potential and produce at their highest level is "How?"

"How do I make sure that gay employees feel safe at work?"

"How do I ensure that the workplace is free of heterosexist, homophobic, and AIDSphobic behaviors?"

"How do I communicate that I value the gay employee and do not want that employee seeking work elsewhere?"

"How much more is there to all of this? What is it exactly that people want?"

Amending the company's non-discrimination policy to include sexual orientation is an important first step. Many companies have done so and without difficulty. The challenge, in the words of people in 12-step recovery programs today, is to "walk the talk." Communicating that we are serious about creating a safe work environment is the task at hand. In order to do so most effectively, it is best to start at the beginning and take a look at the people we are trying to reach. Who, then, are gay, lesbian, and bisexual people?

NOTE ON LANGUAGE

Gay, lesbian, and *bisexual* are words with different meanings. *Gay* usually, but not exclusively, refers to homosexual men; *lesbian* refers to homosexual women; *bisexual* refers to men and women who have erotic/affectional attractions to both genders. Though all three groups of people experience discrimination because of their sexual orientations, each group often has different experiences with self-discovery, with how each conceptualizes and expresses sexuality, and with prejudice. Each group may also have different priorities, personally and professionally. (Likewise, within each group there will be diversity in attitudes and experiences.) To acknowledge these differences, I will use, as often as possible, all three words together in a sentence. Most members of the gay, lesbian, and bisexual communities appreciate this effort. They also appreciate how cumbersome always using all three words can be for the writer and the reader. For that reason, the word *gay* is often employed as a shorthand reference to gay men, lesbian women, and bisexual people. I do so in this book. I also, as often as possible, use *gay, lesbian,* and *bisexual* as adjectives rather than as nouns to underscore that sexual orientation is a part of who we are, as are race and gender, but not all of who we are. More information on the use of these words is in Chapter Seven.

2 / Why Gay People Come Out

ONE OF THE symbols gay people use to identify themselves to one another and to heterosexual people is the rainbow flag. The flag sometimes hangs in front of a home or appears as a bumper sticker. With bold stripes of red, orange, yellow, green, blue, and purple, the rainbow flag proclaims the multidimensional aspects of the gay, lesbian, and bisexual communities. We are gay and black, gay and white, gay and yellow, red, and brown. We are gay and poor, gay and wealthy, gay and fundamentalist, gay and atheist, gay and Republican, gay and Democrat. We are physically challenged, we are young, we are parents and grandparents, we are in nursing homes, we are in the classroom, military, priesthood, locker room, and halls of Congress. We are everywhere—always have been and always will be.

Because we come from such diverse backgrounds, we have different advantages and disadvantages, different skills, different goals, and different values from each other. No one speaks for all of us. The one thing we share in common is our oppression, and even that can be affected by our diversity.

As an example, I consider myself well off. I wasn't always, but I feel I am now. I celebrate who and what I am. I have a lifetime partner with whom I share the bounties of love. I am well paid for what I do. I have a family and a close group of friends who love me. That doesn't mean that I don't face harassment and discrimination because I am gay. I have been screamed at by teenagers in passing cars and by drunken college students out of apartment windows. *Flamer* and *faggot* have been thrown at me, along with occasional death threats, obscene phone calls, and pieces of hate mail. But I can handle those today. I wasn't always able to, but I can now.

My life has been a journey from self-loathing to self-affirmation. When I tell people that I am a gay man, I am telling them who I am, what I have been through, how I survived, where I am now, and *not* what I do. When people say, "Why do you have to tell us you are gay? We don't tell you what we do in bed," it is clear that they do not understand.

The ups and downs of my journey as a frightened, closeted young gay man were influenced by the other factors that made me unique. I grew up in an Irish Catholic household as the middle child of seven. I am the product of sixteen years of parochial education. I aspired to be a saint and was considered by many observers to be "the best little boy in the world." My sense of self, of my lovability, of my chances to survive were influenced by factors that may have been different for my lesbian, gay, and bisexual friends. Yet all of us are alike in that all of us had a secret we were afraid to tell. Keeping this secret is the loneliest and unhappiest of struggles. It separates us from the human family. We wanted and needed to be able to say we were gay.

What is it a man or woman is telling us when they say they are a gay, lesbian, or bisexual person, and why might they feel the need to tell us?

Several years ago, a Catholic theologian asked me, "What's the worst thing about being gay?" A friend of mine chimed in, "It can be forgetting how horrible it was growing up!"

We are talking about children having an awareness of being "different," growing up in a culture that refers to their feelings as "sick," "disgusting," and "immoral." The real horror of being gay is growing up with a secret you don't understand and are afraid to share with anyone for fear that they won't love you anymore.

Sometimes, when speaking with a gay audience, I'll say, "For those of us who were aware of our sexual feelings at an early age, wasn't it almost as if this spaceship came down and placed us in our homes as babies? We always knew we were different and we thought we were the only ones. We learned to speak 'heterosexual' in order to survive. We laughed at the sexual jokes, pretended we were interested in our dates, lied our way through questions about our feelings, and prayed that one day we would get it; one day we would feel what our heterosexual parents and siblings felt." Heads throughout the audience nod in agreement.

"When the gay movement happened," I continue, "we left our houses and gathered together in shock and excitement. Finally, here was someone who spoke my language. Here were people who understood my isolation and loneliness."

The "horror" of being gay is the horror of having a secret you don't understand. How many of us, gay or straight, had a book on homosexuality in our family library? How many of us had a book on homosexuality in our high school library, or had a pamphlet on being gay in the rack outside the guidance counselor's office, or had anyone to talk to or see as a role model? No hands go up when I ask these questions. So how were any of us supposed to understand the secret?

Gay kids wonder, "What does this mean? Why do I feel like this? Did God make a mistake? Did I do something wrong? Will it pass? Can I cure myself? Will Mom and Dad hate me? If I marry the right person, will I be okay? Will I ever be happy? Can I have children? Where will I work?"

Not knowing as a child what your feelings mean can create a terrible burden to carry alone. Fearing the ramifications if anyone finds out your secret can take a terrible toll: "Sissy, fairy, pansy, homo, punk, queen, dyke, lezzie, faggot, fruit, queer."

The Bush Administration's Department of Health and

Human Services received a report on teenage suicide that said that of all completed teenage suicides, 30 percent were gay related. It has been estimated that 1,500 gay teenagers kill themselves every year in the United States. For these kids, being gay was a secret they didn't understand and were afraid to share with anyone for fear that that person wouldn't love them anymore.

I remember as a kid, sitting alone with my private fears that I was bad because of my sexual feelings. Mom came up and said with concern, "Honey, are you okay? You look a little down in the dumps." I, like most every gay person I have ever met, said, "I'm fine." I knew that if I didn't say "I'm fine," Mom would want to know why I wasn't fine. I couldn't tell her because I was afraid if I did she wouldn't love me anymore. For that reason, gay kids who are punched on the playground or teased in the locker room generally don't tell their teachers, parents, or brothers and sisters it happened. Gay and lesbian college kids who are in the closet but who are nevertheless being harassed often don't tell their residence advisor that someone is calling them on the phone at three in the morning, screaming "faggot" or "dyke," and hanging up or pounding on their door and then disappearing in a gale of laughter. "If I tell," these students think, "everyone will then know for sure. Maybe it will pass if I keep my mouth shut." For that same reason, closeted gay and lesbian employees who are subjected to cruel jokes or bigoted statements generally don't say anything but, "I'm fine."

Clearly, many people experience discrimination throughout their lives. Black, yellow, red, and brown children are called terrible names. They are teased and bullied. Such treatment hurts them badly. But black, yellow, red, and brown kids, unless adopted, generally have black, yellow, red, or brown parents who also have been called the same terrible names. Their parents have been teased and bullied too. My parents may have been teased as children, but not for being gay. Like the parents of most gay people, my parents were heterosexual and presumed I was, too.

Because of this, we never talked about homosexuality in my house. My parents never said to me, "Honey, when you are called 'queer' or 'faggot,' when you are threatened or receive an obscene phone call, come home to us because we love gay people in this house." They didn't say this because they didn't know. I knew they didn't know and rightly or wrongly presumed they wouldn't want to know.

"What might it be like to grow up living with such fear and self-doubt?" I ask participants in my workshop. What would it be like to be thirteen years old, sitting next to your dad in the car. The disc jockey on the radio tells a fag joke. You look over, see that your dad is laughing, and you say to yourself, "I will *never* tell him." This is not because Dad is a bad person. He wouldn't laugh if he knew you were gay. He is laughing because he assumes that you, like him, are heterosexual. You fear that if he finds out you're gay, he would think that you're a bad person. You believe this because he laughed at that fag joke.

Imagine being a fifteen-year-old girl who has always felt strongly attracted to other women. Who are your role models? Who can you look at in the movies or on television and say, "Hey, I'll make it. I'll be okay. Look at so-and-so. They are doing just fine."

When I was a kid, the only gay person I ever saw on television was interviewed behind a screen. He was just a shadow whose voice was changed to protect him and his name was in quote marks to let us know it was a make-believe name. That's how we interview mafia hit men and drug dealers today. That was my role model.

My parents said later that they knew gay people. They didn't want us, as children, to meet them for fear that it would influence our sexual development. They did what they thought was best, but in the meantime, I was feeling all alone.

So imagine that you are a fifteen-year-old girl. You think you are a lesbian but also want to have children. You see that Oprah Winfrey is going to have a show on lesbian mothers one afternoon. God bless Oprah! All day long, all you can think about is watching that show. When you get home from school, you turn on the television, hope that no one walks into the room, and you watch and listen more closely than you have ever watched anything in your life. But then Mom walks in. She listens for a minute, walks over to the TV, turns it off, and says, "Honey, I don't want you listening to this." And you say to yourself, "I will *never* tell Mom my secret," not because Mom is a bad person but because Mom thinks these lesbian women are bad.

Fearing the loss of love of your parents because of who you are can be a powerful influence in one's life. You find yourself not trusting their affection because you fear it is conditional. I was a super achiever. I won awards and high praise. I was an altar boy, patrol boy, senior-class president, but no matter what I achieved, I doubted I would be loved if anyone found out my secret. "I'm so proud of you," I would hear from parent, grandparent, teacher, or priest and I would say to myself, as most every gay person I know did, "You wouldn't be if you knew."

When I graduated from high school, the faculty unanimously voted me the John Stewart Christian Leadership Award for "high school scholarship and leadership" and placed my name on a large plaque outside of the principal's office. I was said to be a young man worthy of emulation. I doubted then whether they would have offered such an honor had they known about my secret. Eight years later, I came out publicly. I finally got up the nerve, after drinking a bottle of paint thinner in a failed suicide attempt, to tell people that I was gay. A short while later, I was told that my name had been taken off the high school plaque.

Many gay, lesbian, and bisexual people fear that if they come out of the closet, the same thing will happen to them. They fear that no one will understand what it is they are saying or why it is they are saying they are lesbian, gay, or bisexual. They fear that this lack of understanding will prompt rejection. For them, the horror of being gay continues to be having a secret they are afraid to share for fear that people won't love (and/or respect) them anymore. Some of us who have come out—as my friend told the theologian— forget how horrible it was. We can forget what people who are in the closet are going through.

I believe that when heterosexual people understand in their hearts the journey that gay people must make, it is far easier for most to empathize with the coming-out process. That is why I offer as part of my training an opportunity to spend a few minutes imagining what it would feel like to grow up with a secret you cannot tell the people you love.

Besides sharing with people my personal story of growing up gay, I lead my audience through a guided fantasy. I ask them to imagine a world very different than our own, a world that may not make a lot of sense but which, if inhabited for a moment, will help us understand why I might need to tell people that I am a gay person and help us understand what it is I am saying when I say that I am gay.

A FANTASY

Imagine, if you would, being adopted by a gay couple as a baby. Suspending any judgments or questions about how and why, imagine your feelings if your primary caregivers were either two lesbian women or two gay men. Pick one or the other couple and get in touch with your feelings.

These people love you very much and are proud of you. You love them too and want them to be proud. These men or women nursed you when you were very sick, walked you to your first day of school, taught you to read, bought you your first bicycle. What would that be like?

What would it feel like if these gay people had other children, too—children who identified themselves as gay? Your older brother has a boyfriend with whom he holds hands. You have seen your older sister kiss her same-sex date. What would that feel like?

And what would it feel like if all others thought you were gay, too? Not only do they think you are gay, they expect you to be gay. In a variety of ways, they let you know that if you want to make them proud, if you want to make them happy, if you want to be always welcomed, you will one day bring home someone of the same sex. They are counting on you to be gay. How do you feel and who do you tell how you feel?

Let's leave the house. You are fourteen years old and heading to your first day of high school. Remember that day? You are sitting next to your best friend on the bus. The bus driver has a song on the radio and all of the kids are singing the words to the song. You know the words and you are singing at the top of your lungs, "I'm gay. I'm gay. I'm gay!"

Without figuring out how and why it would work, how would it feel to be fourteen years old, sitting next to your best friend who is gay and who thinks you are too, singing a gay song the gay bus driver has turned up loud on the gay radio station? How would it feel if every song you ever heard was written by one gay person to another? What if every book you ever read, every movie you ever saw, every billboard you ever passed featured the beauty and joy of gay love? How do you feel and who do you tell how you feel?

Now, not everyone is a healthy, happy homosexual. There are people who are thought to be sexually obsessed with people of the other sex. The very thought could make you sick. These people are technically called heterosexuals, but most folks refer to them as "breeders." "Make love not breeder babies," the bumper sticker says. Once, when a local group of breeders tried to get legislation passed so they would not lose their jobs or apartments for being straight, you actually saw a sign that read: "Kill a breeder for Christ."

In seventh grade your best friend whispered in your ear that "God would vomit in the presence of breeders." That same year, someone wrote in Magic Marker on the john wall, "Kelly is a breeder," and no one sat with Kelly all week in the school cafeteria. In eighth grade, the boy suspected of being a breeder was teased incessantly and was always the first one hit in the head with the dodge ball during gym. The girl suspected of being a breeder had her locker trashed on a regular basis. How do you feel and who do you tell how you feel?

Your homeroom teacher is gay. The principal is gay. Your guidance counselor is gay, and the librarian is gay. Everyone thinks you are, too.

On Tuesday night of your first week of school, you are called to the phone at home. If you are a man, Bob is on the phone for you. Bob is a sophomore on the wrestling team and on student council. He wants to take you to the school's first dance of the year on Friday. At the end of the conversation, after you tell Bob yes, he says to you that he thinks you are cute.

If you are a woman, come to the phone and talk to Susan. She is the pretty girl who sits next to you in math class, the one who has been smiling at you for two days. Susan says her older sister will drive the two of you to the dance. You say yes. Susan is thrilled.

The gym is filled with same-sex couples. Initially it is easy because the music is fast. But now it's slow. Slow dance after slow dance has you in Bob's fifteen-year-old arms if you are a man or in Susan's fourteen-year-old arms if you are a woman. He or she is holding you tight, nuzzling your neck, whispering in your ear, "Are you having fun?"

Now you are at the front door. Your anxious but excited date takes you into his or her arms, pulls you close, and kisses you firmly on the lips. You walk inside. Your gay family is waiting up for you. "Sweetheart," they say, "you look like a million bucks. Tell us all about it. Did you have fun?" How do you feel and who do you tell how you feel?

Every day it's the same. To be popular you better have a steady boyfriend if you are a man or a steady girlfriend if you are a woman. Pass them love notes in class; put their name in a big heart on your notebook; go out on dates to gay movies, gay restaurants, gay parties; kiss them; tell them you love them. But what do you feel and who do you talk to? Do you think there might be a book on being a breeder in the high school library? And if there is, do you have the courage to take it off the shelf, hand it to the gay librarian, pull out that little index card in the back, write your name on it and risk that for the next four years someone will walk through the halls saying, "Guess who checked out the breeder book!"

You go to college, hoping things will be different. Please let it be different. In college there is a group of breeders just like you who are brazen enough to have weekly meetings in the student union. But everyone makes fun of them. No one wants to share a room with them. No one wants to sit with them in the cafeteria or have them in their social groups. Some people actually get up and move if a breeder sits next to them in class. The posters announcing their meetings are defaced or torn down. So keep on your mask. Stay in the closet. Date someone of the same sex. You are now expected to wet kiss. You are now having gay sex. Such pressure to conform. How do you feel? Who can you tell?

As a senior you are walking down the street and at the gay newsstand on the corner you see a gay man pointing and laughing at something. He is pointing and laughing at a tiny stack of newspapers that say *Heterosexual News*. There are people with the same sick secret you have who are organized enough to put out a newspaper, and this man is laughing at it. When he moves on, you reach down, grab the breeder newspaper, grab two gay magazines to hide it, put down more money than the three of them cost, don't look the man behind the counter in the eye, don't wait for your change, hurry home to your room, lock the door, think of a hiding place for this piece of trash because if your roommate discovers it you are out on your ear, and read about yourself for the very first time. Read each word carefully.

On page 6 you see an advertisement for a bar located in your college town that caters to people just like you. Every night of the week when you are with gay friends pretending to be gay yourself, heterosexual men and women are gathering in this bar. You decide you have to see for yourself. Not once have you ever met another heterosexual person. What will they be like?

You sneak away from your gay friends and go to the bar. You enter nervously and order a quick drink. Then another. Then another. Fortified enough to look around the room, you see men dancing with women. Men and women are laughing and talking and holding hands and putting their arms around each other. Initially it scares you, but strangely enough you feel at home.

The attractive person of the other sex who has been smiling at you from the other side of the bar finally gets up the nerve to walk over and introduce him- or herself to you, and offers to buy you a drink. You talk nervously at first and then with excitement. You say it is your first trip into a bar like this. "Is it safe?"

"The police used to raid it and take us all down to the station every so often, but they leave us alone pretty much now," he or she explains. "Would you like to dance?"

The next day your gay friends say, "Boy, are you in a good mood. Where were you last night?" All day long, all you can think about is the bar, your new friend, and how comfortable you felt being surrounded by people just like you. You return over and over. You spend a lot of wonderful time with your new friend—with your new love. You can't stand to be apart from your friend. You want to introduce him or her to your gay friends and to your gay family, but you are afraid. You don't want to lose your family or friends, but you don't want to lose your new love, either. Keep your secret.

Eventually, the two of you get an apartment together. It has to be a two-bedroom apartment because the gay landlord would never rent a one-bedroom apartment to a man and a woman. That would be sick and disgusting. Besides, how would you ever be able to entertain your gay friends and gay family? So you stretch your dollars and rent a two-bedroom apartment. You put your possessions in one bedroom and your lover puts his or her things in the other, and you close the shades at night and hide your breeder books and newspapers when you leave for work because you can't risk losing this honeymoon heaven you have found for yourself.

No one at work knows about your friend—not your boss, not your office mate. His or her picture is not on your desk. You don't call each other at work. You attend office social functions alone or you bring a gay date. You panic when people start talking about holiday or weekend plans, when they attempt to fix you up with their gay brother or lesbian sister, or when someone tells a breeder joke.

It's okay. You can survive it, you think. You're fine. It isn't fun, but it's tolerable. And then one day you are walking home and a stranger asks you how your friend is doing. "Did your friend make it?" they ask. "How horrible it must be." You sense tragedy. No one called you. How could they? You insisted that your lover not carry your name in his or her wallet. What if the wallet was stolen? People would find out.

Finally you find your friend on the other side of a plate-glass window in the intensive-care unit of a local hospital. With eyes swollen shut, he or she fights for life alone because no one told you. Your first impulse is to rush in, take his or her hand, kiss it gently, and say, "I'm sorry. No one told me. I'm here. Hang in there. I love you," but you quickly remind yourself that the gay doctors and gay nurses who are attempting to bring back out of critical condition the love of your life presume they are working on a homosexual. What would their reaction be, you wonder, if they knew that this person is a breeder? How would that affect them? Should you do anything that would reveal the secret?

Do you go into the intensive-care unit, or do you sit outside and wait. In either case, can you call your gay boss or your gay office mate and come out at that time? Can you tell them you won't be into work the next day and why? Can you ask that someone come down and sit with you? How do you feel and who do you tell how you feel?

Alone? Frightened? Angry? Hurt? Alienated? Those are some of the words heterosexual people come up with to describe how they felt going through the fantasy. Those are good words, and there are others, that help describe what it is like growing up with a secret you do not understand and are afraid to tell anyone for fear that you won't be loved or respected anymore. Though gay people are all unique, those words are our common denominators. Those are the words we often use with one another to talk about what it was like for us to grow up gay, lesbian, and bisexual.

The guided fantasy helps capture some of the feelings, but there is more to consider in a discussion of who gay people are and why they come out. There are facts and they also enable most people to better understand and respond to a discussion of gay issues in the workplace.

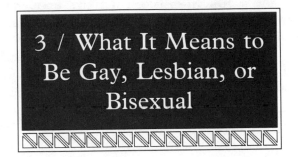

3 / What It Means to Be Gay, Lesbian, or Bisexual

EACH WORKDAY MORNING, Kathleen and Karen leave the home they share as partners in life and head to their jobs in the same corporation. Kathleen is a confident, outspoken leader of the gay, lesbian, and bisexual employee support group. Karen is in the closet.

Occasionally, Kathleen has to listen to anonymous obscene messages on her office answering machine that intend to threaten her because of her involvement with the gay group. Karen never receives such calls, but she does hear fag and dyke jokes from co-workers who think she is heterosexual.

Kathleen is angered by the phone calls but knows how to address them through the company's diversity management and security offices. Karen is hurt, angered, and intimidated by the anti-gay humor and feels she can do nothing but stew or report the horror to Kathleen at home at night.

Karen dreads going to work in the morning. Kathleen looks forward to it, because she feels she has a "family" at work in her gay support group. She says that coming out to her co-workers removed daily stress from her life and allows her to focus her energy on her work. She feels energized.

Kathleen sometimes gets impatient with Karen. She feels that Karen's dread of her co-workers' homophobia could be remedied by Karen's coming out. Then people would never tell her anti-gay jokes. Then she could relax about having Kathleen's picture on her desk. Then she could make and take personal phone calls in front of her office mate, casually discuss weekend plans, attend on-site meetings of the gay employee support group, and never again suffer in silence.

But Karen is afraid that being open about her sexual orientation will mean more hostility. She wants to be like Kathleen—so proud, so in control, so free—but she fears that coming out will mean limited career opportunity.

Kathleen and Karen are the real names of real people. They work in corporate America and they present us with a model for further discussing gay issues in the workplace. By defining terms and offering insights, we can learn to put Kathleen and Karen and the millions of homosexual Americans like them into better perspective.

First, what is a homosexual person? A homosexual person is one whose primary feelings of sexual attraction are for people of the same gender. Easy enough. But do you have to act on those feelings in order to be gay? Do gay people wish they were the other sex? Are gay people attracted to everyone of their gender? Do you choose to be gay? Can you change your feelings? Are gay people the same as transvestites or transsexuals?

From the perspective of a gay person, these questions can feel tedious and demeaning. From the perspective of an educator who works primarily with heterosexuals who have never had the opportunity to discuss this issue, the questions are real and relevant. So let's start at the beginning.

It's helpful to first make distinctions between biological sex, gender identity, gender role, and sexual orientation.[1]

BIOLOGICAL SEX

Our biological sex is the gender (male or female) with which we are born. It is determined by our chromosomes (XX for females and XY for males). It is influenced by our hormones (estrogen and progesterone for females and testosterone for males), and it is evidenced by our genitals (vulva, clitoris, and vagina for females and penis and testicles for males). With a quick look, the doctor or midwife is usually able to say with ease, "It's a girl" or "It's a boy." People do not choose for themselves at birth their biological sex. Our biological sex is not influenced by the culture. While there are some rare exceptions, we are either male or female. Our biological sex is what we are.

GENDER IDENTITY

Gender identity is how we perceive and what we call ourselves. Am I a boy or a girl? Am I a man or a woman? For most of us, the answer is clear and easy, although we may disagree about what it means to be a *"real* man" or a *"real* woman."* People who work in the field of child development tell us that our gender identity is set for us between 18 months to three years of age. This is true for all people, regardless of their sexual orientation.

A person whose gender identity is different than his or her biological sex is said to have *gender-identity conflict* or *gender dysphoria*. No one knows for sure why this happens, and there are perhaps multiple reasons, varying from person to person. A person with such a lack of comfort with his or her biological sex is referred to as a transsexual. Some transsexuals have surgery to alter their genitals to conform to their gender identity. Many people confuse gender identity (how we perceive ourselves) with sexual orientation (our feelings of sexual attraction). They are two separate issues. Studies show, in fact, that the majority of post-operative transsexuals are heterosexual in their sexual orientation.[2] (See Chapter Seven for further discussion about transsexualism.)

GENDER ROLE

Gender role (also sometimes called *sex role*) is what the culture expects of us because of our biological sex. We play a role as a boy or as a girl, as a man or as a woman in response to norms for our gender. Sometimes we are comfortable with that role. Sometimes we are not. Sometimes we go along with the culture's expectations. Sometimes we don't. Sometimes the culture is flexible about the roles, and sometimes the culture severely punishes non-compliance.

Examples of gender role would be the culture's guidelines for boys and girls on what are appropriate toys and games. In my all-boys Catholic high school, we often evaluated the way a guy held his books or the way he walked. You passed or didn't pass the test of masculinity based upon how you threw or caught the ball and whether or not you cried when you got hurt.

Gender role can vary from culture to culture. For instance, men from India who work in American companies tell us that one of the first lessons they had to learn in the United States was not to hold hands with their male friends in public, something in India that was expected but in America punished with ridicule and assumptions about their sexual orientation.

People often confuse gender role with gender identity. Some people think if an American woman wants to be a police officer or serve in combat or play professional sports, she must be confused about her gender because "real women" wouldn't do such things. Likewise, men who are nurses, flight attendants, or dancers are also often viewed with suspicion because some people think "real men" wouldn't be interested in such professions. Narrow concepts of what is an appropriate gender role can cause havoc in the workplace, particularly in a company that employs or serves people from various cultures. If because of our culture or our upbringing we have unyielding beliefs of how men and women should dress and act, non-compliance can cause anxiety and discomfort and we are further handicapped in our efforts to work cohesively and productively with those who are different than us.

People also confuse gender role with sexual orientation. Women who wear "sensible shoes," don't shave their legs or underarms, and don't wear makeup are sometimes thought to be "manly," and therefore lesbian. Men who wear earrings can confuse our sense of gender. People used to think that only gay men wore earrings and, without benefit of accurate information, they concluded that gay men did so because they weren't "real men." Somewhere along the line, they thought, these gay men must have got confused about what it means to be a man. Perhaps their fathers weren't good role models, they guessed. But then straight men started piercing their ears. Does that make them gay? No. Does that make them less than fully male? No, but then, they always pierce the right ear, don't they? Or is it the left?

Gender role often has very little to do with sexual orientation. My fraternity brother in college was, by the culture's standards, an effeminate man. He was tall, lanky, bounced when he walked, had a high-pitched laugh, played the piano, and was presumed by most observers, including me, to be gay. He wasn't and is a happily married heterosexual husband and father. But for the majority of his life, perhaps even today, people erroneously drew conclusions about him and acted accordingly. There are lots of heterosexual people who satisfy society's stereotype of gay people.

Our gender role is what we do, and often it expresses how we feel about what it means to be a "real man" or a "real woman." But it is different from whom we are attracted to.

SEXUAL ORIENTATION

Sexual orientation is that thing, influenced by a variety of factors, that determines to whom we are erotically attracted. Our sexual orientation—heterosexual, homosexual, or bisexual—probably is heavily, though not completely, influenced by genetics and hormones, with some unknown environmental co-factors.

We know more about sexual orientation today than any previous generation, but we don't know an awful lot. We are more sure about what doesn't cause sexual orientation than what does.*

Recent studies of identical and fraternal twins underscore the genetic link to sexual orientation but also reinforce that it is not entirely genetic. Of fifty-six sets of male identical twins, when one was gay, 52 percent of the time the other twin was, too. (Among female identical twins there was a 48 percent correlation.) By contrast, 22 percent of the fraternal twin brothers of fifty-four gay men were also gay (16 percent for females). Among fifty-seven gay men with adopted brothers, only 11 percent of the brothers were also gay (6 percent of the females).[3]

Recent results from Salk Institute and UCLA studies that examined the brains of heterosexual men and women and gay men showed evidence of biological differences, but again the results are only small pieces of the big puzzle. A cluster of cells in the hypothalamus, thought to be responsible for sexual drive, was found to be smaller, on average, in homosexually identified men than in heterosexually identified men, according to the Salk Institute study.[4] At UCLA, researchers found that the cluster of cells that connects the right and left lobes of the brain was 34 percent larger in homosexual men than in heterosexual men.[5]

While many people believe there are environmental factors involved in the development of sexual orientation, no one knows for sure just what they are. Gay people and straight people come from the same family dynamics.[6] We know that homosexuality exists in every species of mammal[7] and that for humans it is probably established very early in

---

* See note on genetics at the end of this chapter.

life, probably by no later than age five.[8] But how and why sexual orientation develops as it does remains unclear.

In fact, there are probably "heterosexualities," "homosexualities," and "bisexualities." In other words, there are probably multiple combinations of factors that influence the development of sexual feelings, and there are varieties of ways we express our sexual feelings and selves. The human condition defies strict, unyielding definitions.

For most people, there is no sense or memory of "choice" of the gender to which we are erotically attracted. Even for bisexual people, their sense of "choice" is not the result of some decision they have made to be attracted to both men and women. Rather, their "choice" is if and how they will express their attractions.

For most of us, there is also no sense that we could change our orientation. Though we know we can change our behavior, even those of us who have worked hard at suppressing the attractions we feel have been unable to eliminate those feelings. Likewise, no one can create erotic feelings they don't have. Like our biological sex, our sexual orientation is "who we are."

In summary, we all have a biological sex. Most of us have a gender identity that is in sync with our biological sex. Those who do not are called transsexuals. Our gender role is how we behave as males and females. Expectations of masculine and feminine behavior are heavily influenced by the culture and are subject to change. Who we are attracted to is determined by our sexual orientation.

Using Kathleen and Karen as our examples, each would be a person born female. That is their biological sex. Each has a core sense of being a woman and positive feelings about her gender identity. As women, the culture has assigned them the same gender roles, yet each of them responds individually to those expectations. For instance, Karen's hair is much shorter than Kathleen's. Kathleen is more assertive than Karen. Karen is softer and shyer than Kathleen. Each woman wears both casual, "sensible" clothing at times and more traditionally "feminine" attire at others. Like all women—lesbian, bisexual, and heterosexual—Kathleen and Karen pick and choose from the list of expected gender-role behaviors. So it is with all of us.

Kathleen and Karen's feelings, behaviors, and actions also help us understand sexual orientation and the important differences among sexual orientation, sexual behavior, and sexual orientation identity.

Sexual orientation—the internal feelings of erotic/romantic attraction—is who we are. There are no choices. It is set at an early age. There is no changing it.

SEXUAL BEHAVIOR

Sexual behavior is what we do. We can act sexually or decide not to. That is our choice. It is also our choice whether to act in accordance with our sexual orientation. Though culture has no influence over sexual orientation, the culture can heavily influence how people will behave. For instance, some people who are homosexual in their orientation will keep their secret and marry persons of the other sex because they are unwilling to pay the price of possibly losing their families, their church, their standing in the community, or their jobs.

SEXUAL ORIENTATION IDENTITY

Sexual orientation identity is what we call ourselves—"gay," "lesbian," "bisexual," "heterosexual." We have both a personal sexual orientation identity and a public sexual orientation identity. For heterosexual persons, the personal and the public sexual orientation identities are almost always the same. For homosexual and bisexual persons, however, because of the often severe penalties inflicted for honesty, a decision about identity must be made. How we identify ourselves is a choice. I may have a homosexual orientation, even act on those sexual feelings, but deny to myself and to anyone else that I am a homosexual person. Or I may acknowledge to myself that I am a homosexual man, but not reveal it to anyone else. Or I may tell my parents that I am gay, but not tell my boss or office mate.

One extreme example of how culture influences both sexual behavior and sexual orientation identity can be found in Nazi Germany. Prior to Adolf Hitler's rise to power, there was a growing movement of support for gay civil rights in Berlin. When the Nazis succeeded in convincing the public that certain groups were polluting the purity of the Aryan race, homosexuals were among those who were rounded up, and sent to their deaths in concentration camps. The pink triangle was the symbol used by the Nazis to label thousands of homosexual prisoners.[9] (This death camp patch is now a sign of solidarity and pride to gay, lesbian, and bisexual communities internationally.) While sexual orientation remained unaffected by the Nazis' ethnic cleansing, such cultural bias greatly influenced the ability of people to behave privately and identify themselves openly as homosexual.

Some people find it helpful to think of the distinctions among orientation, behavior , and identity in terms of "handedness." We know that there is a predictable percentage of people in the world who are left-handed. Parents don't create left-handed children. It happens prenatally (in the womb). Being left-handed is the person's orientation.

The culture can and does influence the behavior of left-handed people. Left-handedness can be so stigmatized that left-handed people learn to write with their right hand and identify themselves as right-handed.

There was a time when left-handedness was seen as a sign of the devil. Left-handed women were thought to be witches. People quoted Scripture to support their bias and essentially forced left-handedness into the closet. Recent studies have shown that left-handed children who are forced to function with their right hand experience major trauma that takes a terrible toll on their development. The same is being said about homosexual people who are forced to behave heterosexually. When our behavior and/or our identity are different than our orientation, it can take a terrible toll.

In working with gay, lesbian, and bisexual people over the last twenty years, I have found that the people who are most open about their sexual orientation experience the least conflict in their lives. They are generally happier in all aspects of their lives than are people who are secretive or in denial. This, obviously, has major ramifications for the business world.

NOTE ON GENETICS

In addition to the important biological studies cited in this section, there is a new genetic study of major significance that was reported in the July 1993 edition of *Science*. Researchers at the National Cancer Institute in Bethesda, Maryland, have just isolated a section on the bottom half of the X chromosome in gay men that they assert is directly linked to male homosexuality. In thirty-three of forty pairs of gay brothers, the siblings had identical pieces of the end tip of the X chromosome, a region designated Xq28. The study strongly suggests that gay men inherit a predisposition for homosexuality from their mother's genes. Research on a similar genetic link among lesbian siblings is forthcoming.

4 / How Gay People Come Out

EMPLOYERS WHO WANT a cohesive, productive work force ideally want gay, lesbian, and bisexual employees who are as comfortable with themselves and with their work world as possible. Though being out of the closet as a self-affirmed gay person does not guarantee productivity, it does increase the chances that the employee is focused, happy, and energized.

To understand why some gay, lesbian, and bisexual employees come out and others feel they cannot requires that we realize that gay people are as different from one another as heterosexual people are from one another. In addition, it is important to know that gay people generally go through stages of self-acceptance. How we go through those stages can be heavily influenced by our family, our friends, our culture, the reaction of the first straight person we told of our sexual orientation, the books we have read, the role models we have seen, our feelings about our appearance, our social skills, our economics, our spirituality, our age, and the environment around us, among other things.

Optimizing the productivity of all gay, lesbian, and bisexual employees requires understanding that the environment of the workplace can heavily influence the movement of gay people toward self-affirmation. Kathleen's partner, Karen, can become a focused, happy, and energized person. Currently she is working through the stages of self-affirmation.

Helping her requires knowing the stages and what influences them.

Australian psychotherapist Vivienne Cass provides us with a very useful model for "homosexual identity formation."[1] Its relevance to the workplace is not only for understanding Karen and what might help her become more productive, but also for understanding why gay, lesbian, and bisexual employees can behave in such different ways.

Why, for instance, do some gay people seem so content with who they are and others seem so unhappy? Why do some gay people satisfy our stereotypes and others seem to blend in? Why would a gay person wear a pink triangle on his or her coat while others shun any political activity? Why do some seem to avoid contact with straight people and some seem to avoid contact with other gay people? Why do gay people seem to become friends with certain heterosexuals, while with others, gay people seem to keep their distance? As a counselor and sexuality educator, I have found Cass's theoretical model a great help in understanding my own changing concepts of self and in understanding those of other gay people.

There are six stages in this model. They describe the probable steps individuals will go through from the first recognition in their lives that they might be gay to the point where being gay is integrated into every aspect of who they are and what they do, including their work. Some people get stuck and never leave the first stage. Some skip stages. Because men and women in this culture tend to conceptualize sexuality differently, gay men and lesbian women often vary in how and when they recognize their erotic feelings for people of the same gender. The same holds true for bisexual men and women.

IDENTITY CONFUSION

Stage One happens when there is continuing personalization of information regarding homosexuality. When a person with a homosexual or bisexual orientation hears or sees things related to homosexuality, such as a gay character in a movie, a gay guest on a talk show, or even a fag joke, it can prompt a sense of recognition: "This feels like it has something to do with me." The more this personalization of homosexuality happens, the more dishonest the person is likely to feel about his or her public heterosexual identity.

For as long as I can remember I knew that I was different. Though as a boy I didn't want to accept that the word *queer* had anything to do with me, I sensed that it did. I was different because I didn't react to things the same way boys my age did. My reaction to Annette Funicello is a good example. Being the first Mouseketeer with breasts that could be perceived beneath her sweatshirt, Annette was the heartthrob of most boys thirteen years old. I pretended to have a crush on Annette so that I would fit in, but I didn't have any feelings for her. Instead, I had feelings for Spin and Marty, two male actors who were Annette's age and also appeared on Disney's "The Mickey Mouse Club." Knowing that I was different but not knowing exactly what it meant, I felt identity confusion.

Accepting the possibility that one might be gay (particularly when you are a thirteen-year-old Irish-Catholic altar boy, patrol boy, would-be saint), was too terrible to imagine. I, like most gay people I know, employed various strategies to deny to myself that this "thing" had anything to do with me. I prayed for help. Others seek a cure on their own, become outspoken anti-gay moral crusaders, become asexual, act out hyperactive heterosexually, shut out any more information on the subject, and so on. Cass labels these denial techniques "inhibition strategies."

Another way of denying that this horrible "thing" has anything to do with me is to employ the "personal innocence strategy." I can do this by changing the meaning of what I feel (or do) or by changing the context. For example, men who have engaged in homosexual activities can change the meaning of what happened by refusing to recognize that there were any emotional feelings connected to the behavior. Women who feel deeply for other women can block the homosexual significance of their feelings by forbidding themselves any sexual content.

If I am unable to accept that what I did might mean I am a homosexual person, I can also change the context of what happened. For instance, I can say things like "I was just experimenting" or "I was drunk" or "I was taken advantage of."

Some homosexual people never leave Stage One. These individuals are sometimes the ones who are most vocal in their opposition to inclusion of "sexual orientation" in the company's non-discrimination policy or in their opposition to the department conducting a workshop on gay and lesbian issues. They are also sometimes the people we can expect to tell or to laugh at anti-gay or AIDS jokes. Many of these people count on the consensus of their peers that homosexuality is wrong in order for them to maintain their resolve not to acknowledge their own feelings. Homophobic people can be heterosexual, bisexual, and homosexual.

Individuals who begin to accept the probability that their feelings or their behavior might be accurately described as homosexual are likely to search for more information on the subject. They may look for books, read pamphlets, or seek out someone with whom they feel they can talk.

Corporations should consider how destructive it can be for homosexual employees to stay stuck in Stage One. Such individuals are often not happy and can be disruptive. People who don't feel good about themselves don't often make good team players. In some cases, the anxiety of denial is so strong that the individual copes by abusing alcohol and other drugs.

Encouraging the existence of a gay, lesbian, and bisexual employee support group is one effective means of enabling individuals to find helpful information. Having gay-related materials in the human resource office or library and training the diversity managers how to be supportive are other important steps a company can take. All supervisors may want to ask themselves, "Would an employee who wants to talk about this issue feel he or she could talk to me? If yes, why? If no, why not?"

IDENTITY COMPARISON

With access to some information, homosexually oriented people can now move into Stage Two. At this point, they have accepted the possibility that they might be homosexual but now need to consider the ramifications. In Stage One, the issue was self-alienation. In Stage Two, individuals face the issue of social alienation. "If I am homosexual, what will it do to my relationships with my family and friends? Will I be able to pursue the career of my choice? Will I be able to get married and have children? Can I maintain an intimate relationship with my church?" How people face these questions is again influenced by a variety of factors, particularly the hostility to homosexuality they feel around them.

If I am able to accept my feelings and behavior as homosexual but refuse to accept that I am really "one of them," I cope perhaps by believing that my relationship with someone of the same sex is a "special case." In this instance, I convince myself that if we ever broke up, I would be heterosexual again. I might also blame the other person and insist that I was seduced. One way or the other, I do not see myself as gay.

Likewise, I might accept my behavior as homosexual but so fear the negative reactions of the important heterosexual people in my life that I devalue homosexuality. Here the individual will often get married to a person of the other sex but engage in same-sex behavior secretly. Or they might choose to move far away from the significant heterosexual people in their lives to protect their secret.

In the workplace, some individuals stuck in Stage Two

may be resentful of those gay people who don't hide who they are. They may join the vocal opposition to domestic-partner benefits because they don't believe gay relationships should be "valued" as equal to heterosexual marriage. Married men who secretly engage in same-sex behavior might feel high anxiety in discussions about AIDS.

Employers can address the disruptive effects of Stage Two by not encouraging and rewarding duplicity by homosexuals who, for whatever reason, are in the closet. If our attitude is that we prefer not to be confronted with a person's homosexual or bisexual orientation, we send out clear messages that secrecy will be rewarded. "If you want to be promoted, keep quiet and play the game." Such a message sabotages all efforts to otherwise create a productive work environment. It is a message that is picked up not only by gay, lesbian, and bisexual people, but also by those heterosexual people whose personal secrets (divorce, inter-racial marriage, pregnancy) cause them to feel cautious and to expend a lot of energy to keep their secrets.

One way of communicating that the corporation values and encourages honesty is to make it clear that all employees are free to bring the person of their choice to company social functions. That means that gay, lesbian, and bisexual employees should feel welcome to bring their same-sex partners to dances, picnics, dinners, and in-house office parties. If this organizational norm can be created comfortably, it communicates to gay employees who are stuck in Stage Two that they have the support of valued heterosexuals in the corporation. It is then easier for gay people to be honest about who they are and to move into Stage Three.

IDENTITY TOLERANCE

In Cass's third stage, individuals have come to accept that they probably are gay and begin to recognize their social and emotional needs.

It is at this stage that people are most likely to call the gay, lesbian, and bisexual employee support group (sometimes anonymously) and ask for information. With their gay legs still a little wobbly, an employee at Stage Three is also likely to ask if the support group meets off-site for fear of being seen by a heterosexual colleague. Stage Three employees probably aren't ready to sign up for domestic-partner benefits, to march under the corporate banner in a Gay Pride march, or perhaps even to enroll in a "Homophobia in the Workplace" workshop, but they are less likely now to be hostile to or resentful of those who do.

Getting in touch with the gay, lesbian, and bisexual communities is important to the individual's developing sense of self. It is in those communities that still-closeted gay men or lesbian women will find role models and will see for themselves how destructive hiding can be. Success at finding such a community and feeling at home in it can depend upon a variety of factors, including the person's sense of their attractiveness, their age, their race, their social skills, and the availability of such a community. It can also be influenced by their employers.

In the corporations with whom I work, some managers encourage all of their employees to attend my workshop, thus making it easy for closeted gay people to learn more about themselves without having to "come out." Other managers, who show no interest in the subject or, worse yet, are known to be hostile, make it very difficult for their gay employees to find community and information. Often, employees must get the written permission of their supervisors to attend the workshop. (The fantasy technique from Chapter Two helps us again here. Imagine asking the gay manager to attend a workshop on being a breeder in the workplace. "What are you interested in that for?")

The quality of the contacts made in the Stage Three search for community affects whether or not the individual will move into the next stage. Some people surround themselves with other closeted people and feel it is good enough to have a small group of gay, lesbian, and/or bisexual friends with whom you secretly meet on occasion. For these individuals, the idea of putting a picture of the same-sex person they care most about on their desk at work, taking personal phone calls in front of their office mate, or attending an office event with a gay significant other would probably be out of the question. The productivity of these closeted gay employees is still being affected by the energy they put into keeping their secret.

If the contacts made in this stage are with self-affirmed individuals who see being gay, lesbian, and bisexual as legitimate, who provide a positive role model for the closeted gay person in search for what being gay means, it is more likely that the individual will move into Stage Four.

IDENTITY ACCEPTANCE

In this stage, people accept rather than tolerate being gay and begin to build a world that supports a more positive identity.

Here again, the heterosexual and homosexual individuals we encounter at this stage heavily influence how we perceive ourselves as gay people in a heterosexual world. When people call or write me for guidance on their journey toward self-affirmation, I encourage them to do two things: (1) Surround themselves with mentally healthy gay, lesbian, and bisexual people who like being gay, and (2) read books by contemporary gay, lesbian, and bisexual authors on all aspects of being gay.

Steve, a gay male leader of a corporate employee support group, told me the reason he came out was because he realized that the gay people who were out of the closet were happier than those who were not. He is a wonderful example of how coming out can affect not only the gay worker's productivity, but also that of others. He reports a change in attitude about going to work. It's now fun for him because he is able to bring together his professional skills and his personal life. He now serves as a role model for gay, lesbian, and bisexual employees across the country who see not only that he is happy and has high energy, but also that he is supported by his management. Steve's positive role modeling has prompted others in his corporation to come out, and they too report increased productivity because it is now safer and more satisfying to go to work.

Kathleen is a positive role model for Karen, too, and helps her see the light at the end of the tunnel. Karen has moved as far as she has come in Cass's stages because of who she is with. Surrounded by less-affirmed lesbians, Karen might have remained stuck in stages Two, Three, or Four. Today, she has one foot solidly in Stage Five.

IDENTITY PRIDE

Stage Five happens when gay people see being gay as fully legitimate and they immerse themselves in the gay, lesbian, and bisexual subculture. (Because in many communities there is not, as yet, a bisexual subculture of which to speak, bisexuals at this stage who identify mostly with their homo-sexual feelings often immerse themselves in the gay or lesbian subculture.) This stage is also marked by gay people having less and less to do with heterosexual people and, sometimes, with closeted gay people.

In this stage, gay employees are likely to join a gay sup-port group and want the meetings held on-site. These indi-viduals are telling more and more heterosexual people that they are gay: parents, co-workers, managers. Stage Five gay employees are the ones most likely to organize "Gay Aware-ness" weeks at work, petition for and enroll in domestic-partner benefit programs, and volunteer to speak as an openly gay, lesbian, or bisexual person during department meetings on diversity issues.

In Stage Five, the combination of pride in being gay and anger at homophobia, heterosexism, and AIDSphobia can create the "activist." Activist gay, lesbian, and bisexual employees may be accused by co-workers of "flaunting" because they wear a pink triangle or rainbow-flag pin, because they speak up loudly against fag or AIDS jokes, or because they want the office-party invitations to indicate the event includes one's "significant other" rather than one's "spouse." These gay employees may also raise eyebrows by talking about their same-sex partner at the lunchroom table or about their participation in a Gay Pride parade.

Because they are spending more and more time in the gay subculture, reading gay books, eating at gay restaurants, vacationing in gay resorts, listening to gay music, the gay, lesbian, and bisexual employees in Stage Five might well appear to have lost their sense of humor or proportion, and indeed, some people in this stage do. They are angry and frustrated by the years they lost to feeling embarrassed by or ashamed of their sexual orientation. Other gay people in this stage immerse themselves in the subculture, see the world as "gay" and "non-gay," but assimilate themselves into their heterosexual work world.

Closeted gay people in the first four stages, can be quite resentful of gay people in Stage Five and vice versa. Those who rely upon the closet for their survival fear that their "brazen" brothers or sisters will "out" them or call attention to them somehow. Those who are out, often forgetting how long and hard their own struggle was, sometimes feel contempt for those who cling to the security of the shadows.

Stage Five, I feel, is an important step in any person's journey, regardless of his or her issue. In this stage, one says, "In order for me to move on with my life, I need to stop and spend a little time tooting my own horn. In the process of tooting, I help convince myself that who I am is good and I help create a world in which people respect me." For some of us, the tooting can become obnoxious. "Enough, already! We hear you. Put down your horn."

Whether gay, lesbian, and bisexual people put down their horn or continue tooting it has a lot to do with the response they get from heterosexual people in their life. If they are convinced that all gay people are good and all heterosexual people are judgmental and rejecting on this issue, they will stay stuck in Stage Five for the sake of survival. Each time gay individuals encounter a rejecting heterosexual parent, clergy person, editorial writer, public official, office mate, or manager, it reinforces their need to stay ghettoized and to continue to make noise. "See, I told you they would reject me. They are as bad as I thought."

If, however, gay, lesbian, and bisexual individuals encounter a heterosexual co-worker or boss who accepts who they are, who doesn't ask them to keep it to themselves, who invites them as they are into their lives, these gay, lesbian, and bisexual people are no longer able to see the world as "gay" and "non-gay," as divided into good gays and bad straights. It is now that gay individuals will move into the final stage of this process.

IDENTITY SYNTHESIS

Stage Six happens when the walls between the world of homosexual men and women and that of "others" comes down and gay people feel their homosexuality integrated into all aspects of their lives. In Stage Six, gay, lesbian, and bisexual people will still feel anger, still feel pride, and still distrust non-supportive heterosexual people, but they will also understand that there is as much diversity in the heterosexual world as there is in the homosexual world, and they will be less inclined to make quick judgments based upon a person's sexual orientation. This, of course, makes them a better team player.

Stage Six is where a company should hope all of its employees end up. At Stage Six, we are unique members of the work force—black, brown, yellow, red, white, gay, lesbian, bisexual, straight, female, male, old, young, able-bodied, physically challenged, worshiping (or not) a higher power in our own private ways—encountering one another with pride, a sense of self, tolerance of difference, and open-mindedness about who might be our friends and allies.

The corporation has far more influence over the development of its gay employees' sense of self and over their ability and willingness to produce than it has ever imagined. Creating a safe environment where such growth can happen requires understanding what it is like to be gay and a familiarity with what stages gay people go through in the process of growth. It also requires taking a look at the enemy. We now need to understand homophobia and heterosexism and how they work together to create havoc in the workplace.

5 / Homophobia and Heterosexism

RON IS OUT for dinner with his boss and male co-workers. During the meal, one of his colleagues interjects a joke he heard on the radio that morning.

"Do you know what G-A-Y stands for?" he asks with an inebriated grin. "Got AIDS yet?"

The others laugh, some nervously. Ron quickly assesses who told the joke, how the boss responded, and whether anyone refused to laugh.

At the end of the meal, the suggestion is made that they all head to the Kitkat Club for the last female strip show of the evening and a nightcap. It's the boys' night out. Why not?

Margaret is sitting with co-workers at lunch in the cafeteria. Beth asks if anyone saw that made-for-TV movie on the Fox channel the night before.

"What was it about?" asks Pam.

"It was about this gay kid who was supposed to get married and tried to kill himself."

"That stuff makes me sick," says Phyllis. "I hate all of this queer stuff. Pat Buchanan is right. Where will it stop?"

What we see in these two stories is heterosexism at work. Heterosexism is the belief that everyone is heterosexual or ought to be.

Ron is a gay man. His lover of six years, Tom, is HIV-positive.

Margaret is a heterosexual woman. Her thirty-year-old daughter, Sally, recently told her that she is a lesbian.

Presuming that Ron is heterosexual, that he wouldn't be offended by the anti-gay joke, and that he would be interested in going to the heterosexual strip joint are examples of heterosexism.

Presuming that Margaret or anyone else at the table wouldn't be offended by a co-worker's disgust at gay people is also heterosexist. Phyllis made an assumption, and as Felix Unger of "The Odd Couple" aptly stated, "When we assume we make an *ass* of *u* and *me*."

When employers put *married* or *single* on application forms, they are assuming that all respondents are either heterosexually married or heterosexually single. When management decides to transfer Bill across the country because he's not married, they assume that there is no significant person in his life who will have to pull up stakes, change jobs, and relocate with him. That's heterosexism.

When the social committee states on the party invitations that employees are welcome to bring their families, they generally mean their heterosexual families—wife or husband and kids. When the boss asks Marilyn, because she's "single," to cover the office during the holiday so that the rest of the employees can be with their families, that too is heterosexism. It assumes heterosexually unmarried people have no family.

Heterosexism is a worldview. For most people, it is probably not even conscious. It is a mind-set based upon limited opportunity to experience diversity. It is also a bias. Because we as individuals are proud to be who or what we are, we think everyone should be like us or, at the very least, should want to be like us.

I am guilty of having had such a bias. As a child, I naively thought all people were Catholic, and if they weren't, once they heard about the Church they would want to be. I recall feeling obliged to remind people that it was Friday, so they shouldn't be eating meat. Mom laughed with embarrassment (in later life) at how she would get phone calls from the neighbors who pleaded, "Virginia, please ask Brian not to try to convert our children to Catholicism."

As a young adult, I learned that not everyone was Catholic or believed what Catholics believed. Further, I learned to my surprise that not everyone liked Catholics. My worldview changed with information and experience. Realizing the existence of Jews, for instance, and respecting their right to believe differently, I became more cautious about my language, such as in not wishing everyone on the street "Merry Christmas" during the last couple weeks of December. It was easier when I thought everyone was a Catholic, but I realize now that I both excluded and offended a lot of people with my mind-set.

Heterosexism has the same effect. The truth is that not everyone is heterosexual. Most of the people who are not don't wish they were, and they value their relationships as intensely as most heterosexuals do. People who are not heterosexual also value their weekends, holidays, and other time away from work. They don't like it presumed they are heterosexual any more than people who are not Catholic like it presumed that they are.

Heterosexism creates havoc in the workplace because it sends out the message that all employees should be heterosexual. For those readers who are heterosexual, imagine for a moment that you are gay and that I am your heterosexual office mate. If I assume that you are like me—heterosexual—I make it difficult for you to tell me that I am wrong. If it is difficult for you to tell me, you will keep your mouth shut and I will continue to assume. I will do things and say things that are inappropriate and sometimes offensive and you won't trust me. Because you have a secret you assume I don't want to hear, you don't feel comfortable with me and don't collaborate as much as you might. That makes it difficult for you to be fully productive and reduces the effectiveness of our teamwork.

As a manager, if I assume that everyone who works for me

is a heterosexual person, I am less likely to be concerned about gay issues in the workplace; I am less aware of the toll of inappropriate comments on homosexuality; I am less inclined to think it worth the company's while to educate employees about gay and lesbian issues; I am less likely to use inclusive language; I am also less likely to hear from gay, lesbian, or bisexual employees about the difficulties they face in doing their job. That clearly would make me a less effective manager.

Fighting heterosexism is like fighting any prejudice. It requires an awareness of the problem, education about the issue, and a commitment to eliminate the problem. This commitment requires, among other things, a diligent effort to break old habits and to use inclusive language.

In many places in which I work, the office party at the end of December is called a *holiday party* and the decorated tree in the lobby is referred to as the *holiday tree* in an effort to acknowledge that some workers are celebrating Christmas and some are celebrating Hanukkah and some don't attach religious significance to that time of year. This is an example of inclusive language. It says, "We respect all of you and don't endorse any one religious belief."

When we say *mail carrier* rather than *postman, chairperson* rather than *chairman, police officer* rather than *policeman,* we are indicating that we understand these positions are also filled by women. Our words are changed to reflect our awareness that language can betray bias. We do the same thing when we refer to adult members of both genders as *men and women* as opposed to *men and girls.* It takes time and practice to change old habits, but when we do, we communicate to everyone listening that we are making the effort to acknowledge and value diversity and to avoid imposing our biases.

In the same way, heterosexist language can also be changed. We can say, for instance, *partner* or *significant other* rather than *spouse.* We can say, "Are you in a relationship?" rather than "Are you married?" If the person is heterosexually married, he or she can say, "Yes, my wife and I . . . " or

"My husband and I . . . " If the person is in a gay relationship, he or she understands that you acknowledge that possibility and will be more inclined to share, "Yes, my partner so-and-so and I . . . "

Although Ray and I have been together in a committed relationship since 1976, if you ask me if I am married, I will probably say no. Because of your language, I would assume—perhaps incorrectly—that you expect me to be heterosexual and that you don't really want to know about Ray.

Recently, a manager asked, "Why do I need to know about Ray?"

I think my boss ought to know about him because our relationship dramatically affects my work life. If he is sick, I may need to stay home. If any member of his immediate family dies, I would want to take time for the funeral. If he has limited vacation time, my vacation plans cannot be easily changed. Because I am in a committed relationship, I may not be willing or able to be transferred. Likewise, if Ray was to be transferred, I would need to be too.

If I am in the closet, my boss and colleagues are likely to misinterpret my reluctance to be open about myself. Though I may be one of the most qualified employees in the department, my performance evaluations may indicate that my "aloofness" serves as a communication barrier. I may seem aloof because I am afraid of engaging in conversations that will either pull me out of the closet or force me to lie. This negative performance review may prevent me from being promoted or even cause me to be fired.

Those are a few examples of why my boss needs "to know about Ray." However, in order for me to be able to share that information with her or him, I need signs that I will be safe in disclosing the information.

In addition to changing language to reflect the diversity of the work force and to encourage trust, heterosexual employees and managers can take other measures to break through the silence that heterosexism creates. For example, commenting casually in appropriate settings about one's own gay friends or offering a positive reaction to a gay-themed tele-vision show or movie will communicate clearly that (1) you know the word *gay*, (2) you know not everyone is heterosex-ual, and (3) you are an "approachable" or "safe" person.

At various AT&T sites across the country, many employ-ees who want to communicate their support of gay, lesbian, and bisexual people or their openness to discussing gay issues are posting "Safe Place" magnets on their office doors, file cabinets, or somewhere else in plain sight. Created by LEAGUE (Lesbian, Bisexual, and Gay United Employees), the company's employee support group, the magnet depicts the pink triangle with a green circle around it. Having a book on gay issues in one's office is another means of communi-cating openness to the issue. Again, it says clearly to all who see it, "This is an issue I care enough about to buy and read a book."

Sometimes people fear that if they communicate support of gay issues, other people will assume they are gay. "When I told my office mate I was coming to this [Homophobia in the Workplace] workshop," one employee confided, "my office mate said, 'Is there something about you you haven't told me?' " This fear of being labeled and possibly subjected to ridicule discourages some heterosexual people and some closeted homosexual people from indicating their interest in or their support of the issue.

"If you don't think that fear is real," I say to the partic-ipants in my workshop, "I have a homework assignment for you. Go buy my last book. It's titled *On Being Gay*." (People in the group begin smiling knowingly.) "Now, I want you to go to your favorite neighborhood bookstore to buy this book and not one that is out of state. And I don't want you to go find my book on the shelf and put other books on the top and bottom of it to make your purchase. I want you to go to the counter and ask for the book by name." (Workshop partic-ipants now begin laughing.) "What's that? You would rather that I send you my book in a plain brown wrapper? You say you will pay me double the price if I'll do so? Why? That's right—we're afraid that if we ask for the book by name, the clerk will say in a loud voice, 'Price check. *On Being Gay.* This person wants the book on homosexuality.' And then what will happen? Everyone in the mall will come out and take a look at the homosexual, because they all think only homosexuals would buy a book about homosexuality!"

Getting in touch with that fear of being suspected of and ridiculed for being a homosexual person helps us better understand what it is like, on a daily basis, to be a closeted gay, lesbian, or bisexual employee. To effectively combat the destructive influences of heterosexism in the workplace requires that we all confront that fear of being labeled.

There is another kind of fear that also gets in the way. Sometimes people fear that if they are supportive, or even tolerant, of gay, lesbian, and bisexual people they will send a false sign that they *approve* of homosexual behavior.

I recently sat with two highly successful lesbian women. One is an attorney with her own law office. Her lover is a partner in a major accounting firm.

"Are you out at work?" I asked the accountant.

"I'm sure my boss knows that I'm gay," she said, "but I'm also sure he doesn't want to talk about it and doesn't want me to talk about it."

The women then told of a recent office social function they hosted in their home for the accounting firm's employees and their spouses. It was a pre-theater cocktail party. Once the boss and his wife finally arrived, all the employees quickly headed out the door with their dates. Joining them was the lesbian accountant who took the arm of her male escort. Her lesbian lover stayed home to clean up the party mess.

When we know that not everyone is a heterosexual person but we believe that people who are not heterosexual ought to be, the mind-set has turned into a bias. That bias creates victims, and victims are less productive. In this case, everyone knows there is a homosexual present but pretends that it isn't so. What gets communicated in subtle ways is "if you wish to continue working with us in a comfortable manner, you will participate in our charade."

It would seem to me that the woman accountant was made a partner in the firm because of her skills in her job. She is an asset to the firm. She helps the company make money. Keeping her happy is important because she is highly productive and not easily replaced. Yet, how long will she be content leaving behind her lover to clean up the party mess? And how long will her lover tolerate her role in this charade?

Often in these situations, where we know that a colleague is a homosexual person but prefer them to act as if they are a heterosexual person, we do so because we are afraid. We fear that by tolerating their difference we will be accepting their homosexuality as equal to heterosexuality; we will be endorsing this *lifestyle*. If we encourage the lesbian accountant to bring her lesbian partner, rather than her phony male date, to the office social event, we fear we will be publicly approving of lesbian sexual activity.

Such "approving" may be contrary to our religious beliefs or our church's teachings, yet Christian managers don't think they are endorsing or encouraging Judaism when they refer to the December office social function as a holiday party. We are not saying everyone should be disabled when we make restrooms wheelchair accessible. We are not saying black people are better than white people when we buy and read books like *The Color Purple* or *The Autobiography of Malcolm X*. This distinction between tolerating difference and endorsing lifestyles is a very important one, and it will need to be made over and over again when confronting heterosexism and homophobia.

Once more, heterosexism is the assumption that everyone is heterosexual or ought to be. Homophobia is different. Homophobia is the fear and hatred of homosexuality in ourselves and/or in other people.

If you think of homophobia on a continuum, at one end we have the violent physical attacks against gay men and lesbian women. Hate crimes against gay people are at epidemic proportions today, inflamed by inappropriate anger about and fear of AIDS.

When I was Boston Mayor Kevin White's liaison to the gay and lesbian community, the mayor had me conduct a survey on constituent needs. Of the 1,600 people who responded to our questions, 76 percent reported they had been verbally assaulted for being gay and 24 percent said they had been physically assaulted because someone perceived they were gay.[1] These alarming percentages have been repeated in study after study at city, state, and national levels.

Most often, the assailant is a male who victimizes gay men primarily with verbal assaults, beatings, and even murder. Some gay men are raped. Lesbian women are more often raped, and they are also victims of verbal abuse, beatings, and murder.

When I first began doing this work in corporate America, I would say, "But we aren't talking about violence in the workplace." Regrettably, however, today we *are* talking about this frightening end of the homophobia continuum being evidenced at work. In one corporation, several people associated publicly with the gay and lesbian employee support group have received death threats on their office telephone answering machines or in letters sent to both office and home. Threats are also made in bathroom graffiti or even, remarkably enough, face-to-face.

At the other end of the homophobia continuum, we have the occasional joke that someone tells at the lunchroom table, the offensive anti-gay cartoon taped to an office door, or the limp-wristed impersonation when talking about homosexuals.

The use of words like *fag, dyke, queer, fairy, pansy, lezzie,* and *homo* to belittle a person is homophobic. Jokes and comments about homosexuals that are negative and hostile are homophobic. Any effort to intimidate a person because the person is gay, perceived to be gay, or perceived to be supportive of gay people is homophobic.

Tony gets off the company's elevator and hears as the

doors close, "I hope you die of AIDS." That's homophobia.

"So you like sex with girls? I'd like to have sex with you and another girl. Call me and we can get it on." That message from a man on Kathleen's office telephone answering machine is also an example of homophobia.

The wall in the office men's room states, "Do your part. Stop AIDS. Smash a fag. Say no to gay rights. Gay rights are the AIDS of society." Here, again, we have homophobia.

Signs with my picture, announcing to employees that I was the company's guest noon-hour speaker, have been defaced. Literature displayed by the gay employee support group has been torn up. The car in the employee parking lot belonging to the openly gay woman was vandalized with deep gouges. These are all instances of homophobia, too.

Having a negative view about the behavior of some gay people is not homophobia, although the intensity of someone's feelings may be fueled by homophobia. One should be able to discuss the riots in Los Angeles after the Rodney King verdict or discuss the settlement by Israel of refugees on the West Bank without being labeled as anti-black or anti-Jewish, unless the discussion turns into a racist or anti-Semitic tirade.

Likewise, people should be able to discuss their feelings about a particular gay group's acts of civil disobedience. People should be able to say, "I don't like the idea of gay people serving in the military." People should be able to acknowledge that the topic makes them uncomfortable. All of this can be done without referring to gay people in negative terms, without indicting the behavior of all gay people because of the behavior of some, without perpetuating stereotypes, without hostility, and with the understanding that not everyone agrees with your opinion.

One of the country's foremost authorities on homophobia, Dr. Gregory Herek, has identified three basic causes for anti-gay bias: experiential attitudes, defensive attitudes, and symbolic attitudes.[2]

EXPERIENTIAL ATTITUDES

One group of people becomes homophobic because of a prior bad experience with one homosexual person that is then generalized to *all* homosexuals. This phenomenon is a common human response that has parallels in racism, anti-Semitism, and sexism. The most effective way to combat this source of homophobia is enabling individuals to meet additional gay and lesbian people, to become more knowledgeable about homosexuality, and to put that bad experience in a context.

DEFENSIVE ATTITUDES

Some people tend to be homophobic because they feel personally threatened by the issue. This cause of homophobia is nurtured by internal feelings of ambivalence or insecurity about one's own sexuality. This group includes those men and women who are wrestling with their own sense of what it means to be a "real man" or a "real woman" and those who are unsure about the direction of their romantic and sexual feelings. As is true in most every other area of life, people who feel good about themselves are not easily threatened by difference. People who feel insecure in themselves are often threatened by all that is different.

High school and college students, particularly young men, are generally my toughest audience because they are going through a predictably insecure period in their lives that is heavily influenced by peer pressure to conform to societal standards of "normalcy." When confronted with difference, such as that found in popular stereotypes of gay men and lesbian women, teens and young adults often react with fear and hatred.

An insecure man's worst fear is that a blatantly "sissified" male will find him attractive. Such a man finds male effeminacy extremely unsettling and suspects that something "unnatural" will be done to him against his will. Though this fear is not based upon fact, it is traumatizing, particularly if the individual has wrestled with any same-sex fantasies himself. The same dynamic can be true for insecure females, though Herek's research suggests, and my experience supports, that heterosexual men tend to have a harder time with this issue than heterosexual women.

Defensive attitudes don't evaporate when the individual enters the work world. Though education and age seem to contribute to a lessening of anxiety and an increase in tolerance for difference, some individuals carry more baggage than others on this issue. Their level of comfort with their gender role and with their sexuality can be heavily influenced by their family background, ethnicity, income level, religious affiliation, and so on.

There is a profile for people who are homophobic: They are more likely to express traditional, restrictive attitudes about gender roles; are more likely to manifest high levels of authoritarianism and related personality characteristics; perceive that their peers have negative attitudes about homosexuality; are less likely to have had personal contact with gay men, lesbian women, or bisexual people; and are more likely to subscribe to a conservative religious ideology.[3]

Remember, this is a profile of people who are most likely to be homophobic and not a suggestion that people who satisfy any of those descriptions will be homophobic. Returning to Herek's category of "defensive attitudes" as a source of homophobia, I find that the characteristic that fits most consistently is the individual who expresses traditional, restrictive attitudes about gender role.

I believe there is a clear link between sexism, heterosexism, and homophobia, particularly for men and women who feel personally threatened by homosexuality. Sexism is the belief that one gender is superior to the other. As most commonly experienced, sexism is the value that it is better to be male than female, that masculine characteristics have more status than feminine ones.

Within the larger Western culture, the degree of sexism varies according to race and ethnicity. The more sexist the culture or subculture, the more strictly defined and enforced are the gender roles. The more strictly defined and enforced the gender roles are, the more homophobic the culture or subculture will be.

If being male is best and being female is inferior, a "real man" is defined as one who is fully male, or, without female attributes. He "thinks" like a man, sharing interest with all other "real men" in such things as excelling in sports, earning a big salary, and being sexually dominant with women. He "acts" like a man, refusing to participate in any behavior thought to be the least bit feminine, such as cooking, doing dishes, nurturing a child, or crying. He "looks" like a man, preferring clothes, haircuts, and even modes of transportation that distinguish him from women.

If one values maleness in such a way and seeks, for the sake of security, membership in the powerful male community, one abhors anything that threatens that image. Homosexuals, particularly homosexual men, more specifically effeminate homosexual men, threaten that image.

Homosexual men are not thought by some heterosexual men to be "real men," thus such words and expressions as *fairy, sissy, pansy, shim, he/she, light in the loafers, poof, queen* are used to describe homosexual men. The very first time most boys pick up a ball, they hear, "Don't throw the ball like a girl" or "Don't throw the ball like a sissy," and the two become interchangeable; being a sissy is equal to being like a girl. Both homosexual and heterosexual men are raised to fear being called *sissy, little girl,* and *queer.* Homosexual men, as previously stated, like being men. However, some homosexual men, as well as some heterosexual men, do not embrace every gender role deemed essential by culture to identify them as "real men." Some appear to be "sissies" or "like a girl." To the insecure heterosexual man, that can be very disturbing.

Lesbian women can be feared and hated by insecure men

and women for different reasons. Insecure heterosexual women can feel defensive toward lesbians because lesbians aren't perceived as buying into preconceived notions of what it means to be "real women." Insecure heterosexual men can be intimidated by what they perceive to be a lesbian's lack of need of them. Some people believe that "real women" need "real men."

Eliminating homophobia that is fueled by this insecurity is best achieved through contact with gay people, education, and the opportunity to talk about one's feelings. Education allows for the dismantling of the myths that exacerbate insecurities. Defensiveness is diminished when individuals no longer feel threatened.

I've noticed, for instance, a change in body language among some men in my workshop when, in talking about myths, I explain that I am not attracted to heterosexual men. Some men who have sat in the back row with their arms crossed and with a scowl on their face all morning sit up and listen more closely after I tell them of one of my first speaking engagements to a heterosexual audience.

It was shortly after I was fired from a job as a reporter and columnist because I acknowledged publicly that I was gay. I was about to speak to a student audience at a local university but was asked by the professor of the class to spend a couple of moments with him in his office beforehand. He began by telling me that because of my appearance and manner he didn't believe that I was homosexual. When I assured him that I was, he hastened to inform me, "Well, I'm not attracted to you."

"I'm not attracted to you, either," I responded politely.

"Why not?"

"Don't you have types?" I asked. "Are you not most attracted to women who look a certain way?"

"Yes," he agreed.

"Well," I said, "I have types too, and you're not my type."

"Oh," he said, a little confused.

"And, besides, you're straight, aren't you?"

"Oh, yes," he said with great pride and conviction.

"I'm not attracted to straight men. I can find them attractive, but I'm not attracted to them," I explained. "I think it would be a waste of time, don't you?"

My being attracted to heterosexual men would be similar to a heterosexual man attempting to date a woman whom he knows is a lesbian. "Well, wait until she meets me," I say in my workshop, pretending to speak for that heterosexual man.

"Forget it," I admonish. "Move on. Get a life."

The men and women in the room laugh together at the stereotypes—at the professor's thinking I should be interested in him because I am a gay man, and at the straight man who thinks he can change the lesbian woman. I believe that such exploration and confrontation of common fears can help people overcome their insecurities and their fear and hatred of gay people

SYMBOLIC ATTITUDES

The third source of homophobia, according to Herek, is prompted by symbolic attitudes. Here, anti-gay bias is fueled by the belief that homosexuality diminishes cherished values. These values, which certainly vary from group to group, give each of us an identity and a sense of belonging.

Opposing gay rights may be required in some people's mind if they wish to maintain ideological purity and/or camaraderie in their group. An example of this would be those people who yearn for a stable family and sense that other supporters of "traditional family values" identify homosexuality as a threat. The intensity of their desire for a stable family can breed fear and hatred of anything they, or others they respect in their group, perceive to be a threat.

Individuals who seek and find community in particular groups, such as the military, political parties, fundamentalist religious groups, country-club social sets, athletic teams, fraternities and sororities, or even one's family, can oppose gay rights and feel hostility to gay people because they perceive they are required to do so if they wish to maintain membership. Likewise, an individual may work for an organization, like the Boy Scouts of America, where homosexuality is perceived by the leadership as contrary to their goals.

In these instances, individuals often parrot what they think they must believe without always examining their own feelings on the issue. Being anti-gay or homophobic in such settings comes with the turf. In some instances, it is used as a test of loyalty.

Challenging such homophobia again involves education. The most effective breakthrough in attitudes comes when respected members of the group challenge anti-gay bias. Oftentimes that education comes from a member of the immediate family. I recall, for instance, reading about a husband and wife who quit the Ku Klux Klan when they learned their son was gay. The mother was quoted in the newspapers as saying she and her husband hated homosexuals until they found out about their son. Hating homosexuals was a value required for membership in the Klan. When they changed their attitude, they changed their values and began to be harassed by their former friends in the Klan. "Now I know what it felt like when we did it to other people," the mother said.

A few years ago, I conducted a workshop at a private school on the issue of addressing the needs of gay youth. As I was preparing to leave the campus, a woman drove up and asked if we could talk. After identifying herself to me as a Born Again Christian, she said that she had resented that I had been invited to speak. She hadn't come into the classroom where I was working because she hadn't wanted it perceived as a sign of approval. But she had wanted to hear what I had to say, so she had stood outside the room all afternoon and listened.

She began her conversation with me angrily, telling me how difficult it was to raise a family these days and how hard she and her husband worked to set a good example for their children. "We believe in the Bible," she said, "and we have always believed that homosexuality is a sin. But I listened to you today and now I don't know what to think. What do I do with you?" I stayed silent. She continued, fighting back her tears, "You touched me deeply today and I'm so confused. I'm afraid to let you into my world. I'm afraid that if I make an exception for you, the whole structure will fall apart. Everything I have been taught and have taught the kids will be challenged. But the truth is the truth and that's what I'm about knowing. I came up here to tell you that, to tell you that I heard your truth, and to ask you if I could hug you." We hugged a long time.

My fantasy is not seeing heterosexual Born Again Christians hugging their gay, lesbian, and bisexual co-workers each morning during the coffee break, though it's not a bad image if one's goal is teamwork. My belief is that regardless of why a person feels hostility toward gay people, such fear and hatred can be diminished, if not completely eliminated. My fantasy, then, is of a workplace where people are free of fear and hatred and feel safe to fully engage in their jobs.

Homophobia, like racism, sexism, and anti-Semitism is not easily eliminated. As previously stated, people in the workplace are entitled to believe whatever they wish but should not be allowed to engage in behavior that creates a hostile environment for their colleagues. A strong company policy that prohibits discrimination is essential. So too is comprehensive education. But the most important ingredient is the determination of the company to recognize and resolve the problem.

To challenge heterosexism and to eliminate homophobic behaviors, managers have to be role models. Employers have to be consistent examples. Rather than delegate this responsibility to the human resource office, everyone in authority, from the CEO on down, needs to become an advocate for tolerance. Persons in positions of authority need to be ever mindful that whether they like it or not, they are constantly being watched and listened to by all employees for the appropriate way to behave in the workplace.

If a manager tolerates inappropriate comments about gay people, if he or she stays silent in the presence of homophobic behaviors, the corporate policy has no meaning in that particular work environment. If a manager provides training for his or her employees on gay issues but does not enthusiastically lead the effort to eliminate heterosexism and homophobia from the workplace, gay people will stay in the closet and continue to be less productive than they could be.

6 / What Gay Employees Want

"OKAY, OKAY," INTERRUPTED the department head. "I can't stay for the rest of this workshop, but I need the bottom line. I can understand the need to eliminate the negative jokes. But is that it? What else do gay people want?"

What gay, lesbian, and bisexual people want is equal and fair treatment in the workplace. Discrimination is not limited to negative interactions at the individual employee level. As with racism and sexism, homophobia also operates at the institutional level. The company's policies, hiring and firing practices, job-performance evaluation methods, benefits packages, and modes of communication (accepted language patterns) often reflect a conscious or unconscious bias against gay employees.

A systematic plan for eliminating discrimination against gay, lesbian, and bisexual employees requires:

1. a specific employment policy that prohibits discrimination based upon sexual orientation;
2. creation of a safe work environment that is free of hetero-sexist, homophobic, and AIDSphobic* behaviors;

---

* Despite the fact that AIDS is a public health issue, primarily associated internationally today with heterosexual transmission, I deliberately add AIDSphobia and the critical need for AIDS education in the workplace to this list of concerns to gay, lesbian, and bisexual employees. Though I run the dangerous risk of perpetuating the myth that AIDS is a "gay disease,"

3. company-wide education about gay issues in the workplace and about AIDS;
4. an equitable benefits program that recognizes the domestic partners of gay, lesbian, and bisexual employees;
5. support of a gay/lesbian/bisexual employee support group;
6. freedom for all employees to participate fully in all aspects of corporate life;
7. public support of gay issues.

Sometimes the opponents of gay civil rights will confuse the issue by insisting that gay people want special privileges or rights. Even very fair-minded people become concerned when they hear these carefully chosen words. No one likes the idea of people taking cuts in line. The words *special privileges* or *special rights* arouse the concern that one group is getting something that others don't have access to. With regard to gay issues in the workplace, nothing could be further from the truth. What gay, lesbian, and bisexual people are looking for is an even playing field. The seven goals listed above help create equal opportunity at work.

NON-DISCRIMINATION POLICY

Having a company policy that prohibits discrimination based upon sexual orientation is an important first step toward equity in the workplace. Without some guarantee from the state, county, city, or employer that there will be no discrimination based upon sexual orientation, gay people have no legal protection against job-related bias.

---

not to include a discussion of AIDS would be a serious and painful omission. As long as misinformed people think that all gay people have AIDS and that you have to be gay to get AIDS, we have no chance of eliminating either homophobia or AIDS. In addition, AIDS has taken a horrible toll on the gay community. The painful sense of loss and the heightened consciousness to the epidemic generally make gay, lesbian, and bisexual people especially concerned about the personal and professional well-being of anyone infected with HIV, regardless of their sexual orientation.

Some people insist that gay, lesbian, and bisexual people are protected against discrimination by the U.S. Constitution, but those people are misinformed. When I was the Mayor of Boston's liaison to the gay and lesbian community, Massachusetts did not have statewide protections for gay people. (It now does.) In my capacity as ombudsman, I was repeatedly asked for help by people who had been fired for being gay or who feared being fired. One such person had been savagely beaten and multiply stabbed because he was gay. The police asked my help in getting him to testify against his assailant, but he was afraid that if he went to court and was seen by someone who knew his boss, he would lose his job as a theater usher. At the time, no one could guarantee him that he wouldn't be fired if he testified.

Not having this kind of guarantee makes most gay, lesbian, and bisexual people extraordinarily cautious. As previously stated, gay people expend enormous amounts of energy hiding their private lives. Having guarantees that sexual orientation is not grounds for discrimination frees that energy for job-related tasks and makes even those gay, lesbian, and bisexual people who choose to remain in the closet feel much less anxious.

The companies and other institutions today that have such a non-discrimination policy cover a broad spectrum from Fortune 500 multinational corporations to religious institutions. Colleges, media outlets, department stores, and municipalities across North America publicly state they will not discriminate against people because of their sexual orientation. Large companies with such policies include Disney World, AT&T, Xerox, 3M, Digital, Bellcore, U.S. West, Kodak, Chase Manhattan Bank, and Procter and Gamble, to name only a few. States with such employment protection include California, Connecticut, Hawaii, Massachusetts, Minnesota, New Jersey, Vermont, and Wisconsin. In most instances, the words *sexual orientation* were merely added to existing non-discrimination policies.

The founder and former president of Digital Equipment

Corporation, Kenneth Olsen, made very clear the scope of his company's intentions when he stated, "It is the policy of the Digital Equipment Corporation to ensure that all employees and candidates for employment are considered for all positions on the basis of their qualifications and abilities, without regard to race, color, sex, religion, age, national origin, citizenship status, veteran status, sexual orientation, or disability. We shall recruit, hire, upgrade, train, and promote all employees in all job classifications, and ensure that all personnel actions such as compensation, benefits, company-sponsored training, tuition assistance, and social and recreational programs are administered without regard to these differences. We will provide a work environment free from discrimination and harassment of any kind.

"Moreover, we are committed to valuing diversity because it is our firm conviction that an environment which embraces difference is critical to each employee's ability to succeed and to the success of the Corporation. . . .

"The Manager of U.S. Equal Opportunity and Affirmative Action will ensure that the intent and practice of this policy are carried out. However, we expect every manager, supervisor, and employee to take an active part in putting these principles into practice—with each other, and in our relationships with customers, vendors, and others with whom we do business."[1]

It is very important to make such a clear statement about the company's policy. According to a 1993 survey by the Society for Human Resource Management, 63 percent of their respondents say they have policies that prohibit discrimination based on sexual orientation. Of that number, however, only 38 percent have it in writing.[2]

Some businesses that don't have a specific written policy insist that they don't discriminate. Sometimes these companies state that their gay employees are already covered by local ordinances or are already covered by broad interpretations of their sexual harassment prohibitions. A public-relations spokesperson for a major automotive company told me, "We don't discriminate against homosexuals and we don't have a policy. We don't discriminate against people who wear bow ties either, and we also don't state that in our policy."

It is not enough, however, for spokespersons to simply say that the company doesn't discriminate against homosexual people. It is essential that the policy be spelled out for everyone to see. Even if they are already protected by state or local ordinances, lesbian, gay, and bisexual employees need to see the words *sexual orientation* in their company's policy. The words say clearly, "We are talking about you. We care about you." It also makes the policy clear to any other employee who may have doubts about the company's intentions.

I recommend that the policy use the words *sexual orientation* instead of *sexual preference*. With this issue, where misunderstanding and misinformation abound, it is very important to be precise. The phrase *sexual preference* suggests to some people that a choice has been made, where in fact none has been. I may prefer chocolate ice cream to vanilla, but I am not oriented toward chocolate ice cream. I have a choice about which flavor to consume. The words *sexual orientation* help reinforce a more accurate picture of gay and lesbian people and of the issue as most social scientists understand it.

If eliminating heterosexism and homophobia from the workplace is an objective, the most important first step, then, is going on record with the clearest language possible that discrimination will not be tolerated. Once stated, the company policy should be widely disseminated. It should appear unabridged in all appropriate publications and forms. All human resource managers should be informed of the company's policy and of management's intention to enforce it. Compliance should be the responsibility of every manager, supervisor, and employee.

It probably goes without saying that the corporation with the specific, widely publicized non-discrimination policy has a much better chance of attracting and keeping talented gay, lesbian, and bisexual workers than the company that makes comments comparing the employment needs of gay people to those who wear bow ties. It is also true that the company that enforces its non-discrimination policy commands more respect and loyalty from its gay employees—and its gay customers—than the one whose policy is considered window dressing.

A SAFE WORK ENVIRONMENT

Enforcing the company policy addresses the second issue raised here: Creation of a work environment that is free of heterosexist, homophobic, and AIDSphobic behaviors. (As a reminder, heterosexism is the bias that everyone is heterosexual or ought to be. Homophobia is the fear and hatred of homosexuals. AIDSphobia is the fear and hatred of AIDS, of people who are HIV-positive and of people who are thought to be at high risk of contracting the disease. As described previously, such bias and fear-based behaviors cause havoc in the workplace and take a terrible toll on productivity.)

There are both proactive and reactive measures that can be taken to enforce the company's policy to protect employees from discrimination and to help create a safe work environment.

Reactive measures are taken in response to violations of the letter and spirit of the policy. Examples of reactive measures would be confronting a person who is telling homophobic jokes or making inappropriate comments about gay people or people with AIDS; immediately removing offensive graffiti from restroom walls and monitoring whether such hostile comments reappear with any pattern; tracing threatening telephone calls made to gay employees and taking appropriate disciplinary actions against the perpetrator. Swift, consistent, and sincere responses to any and all violations will communicate to everyone that the company means business. It is particularly important that the response to anti-gay bias be equal to the company's response to racist, sexist, or anti-Semitic bias. Gay people are not looking for special attention, just equal attention.

Sometimes, however, equal attention requires a special sensitivity. This is certainly the case in dealing with issues like sexual assault. For example, police officers learned through experience that if they hoped to get women to come forward and report rape, a change in procedure would be required. The women would need to be interviewed in private as opposed to questioned like other victims of crime, in front of a roomful of officers, as often happens. The special sensitivity shown in this instance has had a dramatic impact on the effectiveness of the police with victims of rape.

Special sensitivity will sometimes be required in addressing anti-gay bias, too. If a gay, lesbian, or bisexual person must "come out" in the company in order to have anti-gay bias addressed by his or her supervisor or diversity manager, the gay person may choose to endure the harassment in silence. This is not in the best interest of the employee or of the company. If he or she does not speak up, the harassment will continue and productivity is affected. In designing the means by which employees can file grievances, the company should show special sensitivity to the need for a safe, confidential procedure.

Proactive measures can also be taken to guarantee compliance with the letter and spirit of the company's non-discrimination policy. These measures are those in which a person or company takes the initiative before problems occur to help create a climate that acknowledges and supports the rights of gay, lesbian, and bisexual employees. For example, an individual can attend and encourage others to attend a workshop on gay issues in the workplace; join—as a heterosexual ally—the gay, lesbian, and bisexual employee support group; attend gay- and AIDS-awareness events such as those featuring speakers or films; write letters to the company newsletter or local newspaper in support of gay people and of those persons with AIDS; display in one's office signs of support, such as the "Safe Place" magnet developed by the gay employees at AT&T; discuss gay issues in a positive manner when appropriate; alter one's language to be inclusive of gay people (for example, saying *significant other* or *partner* rather than *spouse*); offer moral support to gay colleagues and to those who are HIV-positive; encourage gay colleagues to bring their significant others or partners to a social event; attend a social event in the home of a gay coworker; read materials of interest to and supportive of gay people.

The company can take proactive measures, too. These include providing training for all employees on gay issues and AIDS; guaranteeing equal pay for equal work; supplying resources to the gay, lesbian, and bisexual employee support group; featuring gay issues in the company newsletter; offering guidelines to all in-house and guest speakers and consultants that encourage inclusive language and prohibit homophobic or AIDSphobic humor; promoting qualified openly gay people to positions of responsibility; reprimanding employees who exhibit hostile attitudes toward gay people; making sure that the company library or diversity management office has up-to-date resources on lesbian, gay, and bisexual issues, such as periodicals, books, and audiovisuals; sponsoring Gay and Lesbian Awareness Week and including gay people in Diversity Awareness Week; ensuring if employees are asked to donate annually to charity that gay- and AIDS-oriented charities are presented as options; refusing to contribute to charities that exclude gay people from their efforts or from employment; and guaranteeing that gay, lesbian, and bisexual people feel welcome to fully participate in all corporate social events.

These examples are not different than those offered to corporations that ask, "How do we make sure our African-American employees, our Hispanic employees, our women employees—and customers—feel valued and included?"

COMPANY-WIDE EDUCATION

To eliminate heterosexist, homophobic, and AIDSphobic behaviors from the workplace, the company needs to provide training for all of its employees. Once again, the precedent set in dealing with racism, sexism, and other issues should be the company's guideline. Unnecessary resentments can be avoided when the response to the concerns of all groups affected by bias is consistent. If training on race issues is optional, it stands to reason it should be optional on homophobia. If training is mandated for other diversity issues, employees should be required to attend sessions on gay issues and AIDS, too.

The advantages of requiring or "strongly encouraging" employees to attend such a training rather than merely offering it as an option are that: (1) people who most need the education but otherwise might not attend are able to gain new insights; (2) closeted gay, lesbian, and bisexual employees who might otherwise fear that their mere presence in the workshop would betray their identity have an excuse to attend; and (3) all levels of workers receive the same information and the same message of support from management.

At Bell Communications Research (Bellcore), where I initiated my workshop, one vice president "strongly encouraged" his 2,500 employees to attend. In so doing, he sent a powerful message to all of his employees that this was an issue he took very seriously. He began by sponsoring the day-long workshop for all of his managers. They, in turn, were encouraged to do the same for the employees in their areas of responsibility. Most of this vice president's employees have now been through the training, establishing for the majority of people in that work group an understanding of the issue, a sense of confidence in themselves to address the topic, and a sense of pride in their management for leading the way on a difficult issue.

At AT&T I was invited to speak at the Chief Financial Officer's organization monthly leadership team meeting. As a result of our time together, each executive decided to sponsor the workshop for his or her organization. In opening each training session, these officers talk of why they feel such a workshop is needed and they underscore their personal commitment to creating a safe work environment for all employees. By doing so, they make clear management's position and set a positive tone for the training.

Education on this issue is the most effective means of breaking through the anxiety that often surrounds the topic of homosexuality. The following responses on a post-workshop evaluation of a session for Bell Laboratories managers are typical of the feedback this kind of training regularly receives.

"I was working from an uninformed position."

"It gave me a sense of courage that is built on information on the subject. I feel that I can now proactively deal with the subject."

"I had never really thought about any of the issues that were presented and I feel bad about that."

"I feel much more comfortable in discussing the subject with others."

Workshops on homophobia and on AIDS should be part of the menu offered to employees by the affirmative action, diversity management, human resource, or education and training offices. It is not enough to include a reference to homosexuals in workshops on "managing diversity," although gay people should certainly be included in any listing of oppressed groups. Even when given four hours of information during my half-day training, many people complain that they needed more time.

There are many highly qualified individual consultants available to conduct trainings on the issues facing gay, lesbian, and bisexual employees, and many major consulting firms are now including components on homophobia. In-house trainings are also being effectively presented in a number of companies. (Guidelines for providing such training are offered in Chapter Eight. Additional resources are suggested in Appendix A.)

AIDS education, which is also badly needed, is best offered as a separate training. AIDS is a public-health and business issue deserving special attention because of its effect on the corporation financially (health-care costs) and in productivity (lost time). AIDSphobia is also a business issue because it takes a terrible toll on the morale of the work force and exacerbates other issues, such as homophobia and racism. (Graffiti in some employee restrooms read, "Help Stomp Out AIDS—Kill a Queer" and "Help Stomp Out AIDS—Kill a Nigger.")

Despite all of the information on AIDS that has been published, many people today remain confused about transmission of the virus and how to prevent it. I find that many participants in my workshop are hungry for accurate information about AIDS, particularly those who are afraid of contracting the disease at work and those who have lost a colleague and/or friend to the disease. A basic course in AIDS that describes how the virus is spread and discusses how the issue impacts the workplace helps not only lower the risk that an employee will be infected but also lessens the impact of AIDSphobia. Such a training, which can be secured by contacting a local AIDS-service organization or by calling the Department of Public Health, also prepares employees for the possibility of working with a colleague who is HIV-positive. (See Chapter Seven for AIDS-training guidelines and Appendix A for resources.)

EQUITABLE BENEFITS PROGRAM

One of the biggest issues on the minds of most gay, lesbian, and bisexual employees, particularly those who are open about their sexual orientation, is that of receiving equal compensation for equal work. A good-faith effort to provide domestic-partner benefits for gay and lesbian employees is an essential ingredient in the company's mission to create an equal playing field where each employee feels valued.

Having domestic-partner benefits means that the partners of gay, lesbian, and bisexual employees would receive the same benefits from the company that are given to the married spouses of heterosexual employees. Beyond the obvious economic benefits represented here, there is an important symbolic value to gay employees. A commonly heard phrase in this discussion is "Equal pay for equal work."

When asked to explain the issue of domestic-partner benefits to employees in my workshop, I created the following scenario:

"Larry," I said to the executive sitting in the front row, "let's pretend that you and I went to the same university, pursued the same studies, graduated with the same grades and honors, and were recruited by the same corporation. We share an office. We do the same work. We are both hailed as the best and the brightest employees in the company. You get married. The next day your wife receives health-care benefits from the corporation. My partner, Ray, with whom I share my life, gets nothing. Because of all of the benefits your wife receives, you are getting paid more than I am to do the same job. I believe that is unfair. It is not fair to me. And it is not fair to our heterosexual co-workers who for whatever reason are not married to the person with whom they share their lives."

"You're right," agreed Larry. "It's not fair."

Same-sex couples cannot legally marry in the United States.* (In some countries, such as Denmark, they are allowed to do so.) While a handful of cities, such as New York, permit gay and lesbian couples to register as partners, the gesture is without much substance. Despite how long, faithfully, and lovingly they have shared their lives with a person of the same sex, gay men and lesbian women are denied the

---

* See note on marriage at the end of this chapter.

legal protections and incentives associated with marriage. Because they cannot legally marry, gay and lesbian employees have not been able to qualify for the spousal benefits provided by their employer. When the company provides domestic-partner benefits to gay employees, it addresses the inequity in workplace compensation.

Some companies have decided to extend benefits to the domestic partners of all of their unmarried employees. Other companies have decided to extend benefits only to gay and lesbian employees who can not legally marry. These companies generally refer to this compensation as spousal-equivalent benefits.

Domestic-partner or spousal-equivalent compensation covers a broad range of benefits from medical and dental insurance to health-club membership. The medical and dental insurance, often referred to as "hard" benefits, can be more difficult to provide, particularly when the company is insured by an outside vendor. Some outside insurance vendors have balked at covering the domestic partners of gay employees because they fear it would be too expensive. (The experience of companies that provide "hard" benefits have shown those fears to be unsubstantiated.)

Some domestic-partner benefits, such as bereavement and family leave, often referred to as "soft" benefits, require no outside negotiation with insurance vendors and can be implemented immediately. In 1988, for instance, the Attorney General of Massachusetts issued these inclusive parameters for state employees regarding family leave:[3]

"Family leave is the time granted from work to employees upon the serious health condition of a dependent child, parent, spouse, named partner, parent of spouse or named partner, or any individual who fits the definition of a dependent under the IRS tax code."

The attorney general's guidelines for bereavement leave state: "Employees can take a leave of up to four calendar days with pay in the case of a death in their families (spouse or named partner, child, parent or parent of spouse or named partner, sibling, grandparent, grandchild) or person living in the employee's household."

Other domestic-partner or spousal-equivalent benefits that require no outside negotiation with insurance vendors include pension plans, relocation expense reimbursement, tuition, access to company facilities, discounts, health-club membership, and those other perquisites that are provided to the spouses of heterosexual employees.

Where companies are self-insured, they can also provide health insurance and dental insurance to the domestic partners of their gay, lesbian, bisexual, and unmarried heterosexual employees. Even when not self-insured, companies can find outside vendors who are willing to cover the domestic partners of "unmarried" employees. (For a current list of these insurance vendors, contact Lambda Legal Defense and Education Fund, cited in Appendix A.)

An ever-increasing number of corporations, organizations, and municipalities provide a range of domestic-partner benefits to their employees. Those corporations that provide both hard and soft benefits include Microsoft, Lotus Development, Apple Computer, Levi Strauss, MCA, Viacom, Sun Microsystems, Ben and Jerry's Homemade, and Montefiore Medical Center, to name only a few. The domestic partners of all gay employees of Boston, Seattle, and West Hollywood, among others, receive some form of domestic benefits. The American Friends Service Committee, the American Psychological Association, and the Episcopal Diocese of Newark, New Jersey, are among the many organizations that have such compensation.

As these corporations and organizations have found, the cost to the company is no more than it would be to add the spouse of a heterosexual employee. In fact, since most gay and lesbian couples are two-income families, both generally insured by their own employers, only a small percentage of gay employees have actually signed up for domestic-partner benefits. Those who do are often without children, which also makes their benefits package less costly than that of the average married heterosexual worker.

A nationalized program of health care, as is provided in Canada, may make the issue of medical insurance for domestic partners moot. Much of the discussion today on medical benefits for the domestic partners of gay male employees has focused on the expense, often fanned by fear of AIDS. Some employers have worried aloud that covering the health-care costs of more gay people would mean major AIDS-related expenses, yet those ill-founded fears have not been realized. Such fears betray a misunderstanding about AIDS, who gets AIDS, and how many people are HIV-positive. It also betrays misinformation about the cost of treating the disease. Should the domestic partner of a homosexual or heterosexual employee need HIV-related treatment, the cost to the insurer is less than it would be for chronic heart problems or cancer.

To qualify for domestic-partner benefits from their company, gay, lesbian, or bisexual employees generally must sign an affidavit testifying that they are involved in a committed relationship. The city of Berkeley, California, for instance, extends a variety of benefits to the domestic partners of all of their municipal employees, regardless of gender. To qualify, the employee must file an Affidavit of Domestic Partnership with the city. In the statement, they swear that:

1. The two parties have resided together for at least six months and intend to do so indefinitely.
2. The two parties are not married, are at least eighteen years old, are not related by blood closer than would bar marriage in California, and are mentally competent to consent to the contract.
3. The two parties declare that they are each other's sole domestic partner and they are responsible for their common welfare.
4. The two parties agree to notify the employer if there is any

change in the circumstances attested to in the affidavit.
5. The two parties affirm, under penalty of perjury, that the assertions in the affidavit are true to the best of their knowledge.

As explained in a memo from Lambda Legal Defense, a gay public-interest law group, the domestic partnership may be officially ended by one of the two parties upon filing with the Risk Management Office a statement, under penalty of perjury, that the partnership is terminated, and a copy of the termination statement will be mailed to the other partner unless both have signed the termination statement. After the termination of the partnership, the employee must wait six months before filing another Affidavit of Domestic Partnership.

Should the employer suffer a loss because of a false statement of domestic partnership or because of failure to notify of a change of circumstances, the employer may bring a civil action to recover losses and reasonable attorney fees.

"Excuse me," said a workshop participant who waved his hand for attention after I had explained the reasoning behind domestic-partner benefits. "I believe that the company giving benefits to your gay partner puts your relationship at the same level as mine, and that's not right. Many of the problems we face today as a society are due to the breakdown of the family. We need to support heterosexual families. We need heterosexual families, or the world will end. Putting your relationship on a par with my family undermines heterosexuality, and I don't think this company ought to be endorsing the gay lifestyle. No offense intended."

"No offense taken," I said. "That's why we're here—to talk about these issues. I agree that the family needs to be supported. I agree that we need heterosexual unions. No gay person I know is arguing otherwise. But how does paying a gay person in a committed relationship the same as we pay a heterosexual person who is married undermine the value and the need for marriage? Are we assuming that if gay people are treated equitably that heterosexuals will decide not to marry? Do I need to be discriminated against in order for a heterosexual to feel his or her marriage is valued?

"You sometimes hear people say that by granting civil rights to homosexuals or by providing domestic-partner benefits the company is endorsing a lifestyle. To begin with, there is no one gay 'lifestyle,' any more than there is a heterosexual 'lifestyle.' It seems to me, though, that when you reward people for being heterosexually married by providing them with an assortment of benefits that unmarried heterosexuals do not receive and that gay people—who can't legally marry—do not receive, the company is discriminating on the basis of both marital status and sexual orientation. Furthermore, it's undermining the reasoning for providing benefits."

As explained to me, corporate benefits have two basic purposes: (1) to enhance the overall compensation package in order to attract and retain the very best employees, and (2) to cushion the impact of personal and family crises in order to reduce their adverse effect on an employee's job performance. By providing domestic-partner benefits to gay, lesbian, and bisexual employees, a company satisfies those two purposes. Such benefits make working for one company more attractive to talented gay people than working for another that has no benefits. Likewise, knowing that their savings will not be wiped out to pay for their partner's recovery from a possible illness reduces unnecessary stress and enables gay employees to focus on their work.

When MCA Inc., a unit of Matsushita Electric Industrial Co. and parent of Universal Studios, extended health-insurance coverage to the partners of its gay and lesbian employees, company president Sidney Sheinberg stated that the policy "underscores MCA's ongoing commitment to create a workplace free of discrimination by ensuring fair treatment of all employees regardless of sexual orientation."[4]

Lotus Development issued a similar statement when they announced they would fully extend domestic-partner benefits. "Lotus recognizes that lesbian and gay employees do not have a choice to legalize permanent and exclusive relationships through marriage; thus they cannot legally share financial, health, and other benefits with their significant partners. For this reason, in the interest of fairness and diversity, Lotus will recognize the significance of such relationships by including them in our policies and benefits."[5]

EMPLOYEE SUPPORT GROUP

The next need articulated by many lesbian, gay, and bisexual employees is for an employee support group. Like those formed by and for African Americans, Hispanics, Asians, women, and others, the groups serve a variety of important functions. They facilitate personal and professional networking and socializing, thus countering the work-related effects of isolation. They also serve the corporation as valuable advocates on the issues of concern to their members.

There are gay and lesbian employee support groups in numerous companies, such as Pacific Gas and Electric, Xerox, Lockheed, Digital, Disney Studios, Boeing, Microsoft, Time/Warner, RAND Corporation, Hewlett-Packard, Sun Microsystems, U.S. West Communications, Levi Strauss, and AT&T, to name but a few.

As cited in previous chapters, the AT&T group is called LEAGUE. As of 1994 there were more than one thousand members in twenty-five LEAGUE chapters across the country. Their vision statement provides a look at how gay, lesbian, and bisexual employee support groups see themselves: "We will foster a work environment that is inclusive and supportive of lesbian, bisexual, and gay employees so these employees can perform freely to their fullest potentials. Our impact will extend to our families, friends, and colleagues as well as customers, suppliers, investors, and the worldwide communities in which we live and work. We commit ourselves to creating a world where differences are respected and valued and where lesbians, bisexuals, and gays will continue AT&T's quest for excellence."

LEAGUE further states that it is their mission to:

- advocate lesbian, bisexual, and gay employee concerns;
- sponsor educational and cultural programs on lesbian, bisexual, and gay issues;
- serve as a liaison between employees, management, and community support groups;
- promote a sense of community among our members.

LEAGUE cites as their "strategic imperatives" to:

- work aggressively toward changing harassing behaviors through education and awareness programs;
- assure that all business units and divisions fulfill AT&T's EEO policy of non-discrimination;
- secure recognition in policies and practices for domestic partnerships and non-traditional families;
- recognize contributions made by lesbian, bisexual, and gay employees at AT&T;
- advertise and sell AT&T products and services directly to lesbian, bisexual, and gay markets.

The support that groups like LEAGUE and others need from their companies is no different than that given to similar employee groups. It includes recognition; participation of a management "angel" who will advocate for the group when necessary; meeting space; financial support to sponsor awareness events; participation of management and co-workers in awareness events; financial support to attend workshops and professional development conferences; access to company newsletters and computer services; representation at corporate discussions or events concerning diversity, benefits, or any other topic for which their input is appropriate.

I believe that companies profit a great deal from the existence of gay employee support groups. These groups keep the company focused on the important issues to gay, lesbian, and bisexual people and serve as a resource for materials and information. Such groups provide safety nets for gay employees who are disenfranchised and don't know how, or feel unable, to utilize employee services. Gay employee support groups provide role models for people struggling with issues of self-esteem. They empower employees to integrate their personal lives into their work in a healthy way. These groups also make the company more attractive to talented gay, lesbian, and bisexual employees from other companies. Knowing there is an immediate source of business contacts and potential friends is an incentive, particularly for people moving into a new geographical area.

PARTICIPATION IN CORPORATE LIFE

Another need articulated by gay employees is the ability to participate fully in all aspects of corporate life. Though not all gay, lesbian, and bisexual employees want to go to the company picnic or to the holiday dance, those who do are looking to management to help make it possible. If gay employees have the interest and the skills to participate in the company's softball or bowling league, they feel they should be able to do so.

The treasurer of one major corporation introduced me and the topic of my talk to his colleagues by saying that he thought of the employees as a *family* and he wanted every member of the family to feel valued. Using that analogy, I would expect my family to invite me to all social family functions if they want me to believe that I am valued. If my heterosexual brothers, sisters, and cousins are able to bring their significant others, so too should I. If a family photo is to be taken and all in-laws are included, so too should my partner, Ray. If every in-law receives gifts or greetings on their birthdays, I would expect that Ray would, too. I don't want to be treated in a special way; I want to be treated equally. (I am delighted and proud to belong to a family in which Ray and I are valued as equal members.)

If gay employees are truly valued members of the work force, they don't expect to be treated in a special way, but equally. If their companies are extending invitations to all employees to participate in an activity, gay, lesbian and bisexual co-workers should feel completely welcome. If companies truly want full participation, gay people, like everyone else, need to feel wanted.

Designing events that will appeal to all employees is an important first step. Using language that is inclusive to encourage participation (*significant other* versus *spouse*) is essential. Sensitivity to aspects of the event that might be offensive to gay employees is also important. For instance, most companies today are careful not to schedule a social event at a "white members only" club. There are parallels for gay people. National boycotts have been held against products, groups, and states that discriminate against gay people, such as the Cracker Barrel Restaurant* chain. People who plan company social functions should seek input from the gay employee support group regarding such possible conflicts.

While management may be concerned that the presence of gay co-workers with same-sex dates at a company social function will make some employees and guests uncomfortable, the company has more to gain than lose by being inclusive. The

---

* Cracker Barrel Old Country Store, Inc., a fast-growing chain of 120 restaurants with nearly 14,000 employees in 16 states, announced in January 1991 a new employment policy that bars people "whose sexual preferences fail to demonstrate normal heterosexual values, which have been the foundation of families in our society." At least eleven gay and lesbian employees were summarily fired. In response to media coverage and protests, the policy was rescinded, but the company never rehired the dismissed employees. Instead, it defended its anti-gay policy by saying it was "a well-intentioned overreaction to the perceived values of our customers and their comfort levels with these individuals." A boycott of the restaurant chain is being observed by consumers who want a good-faith effort from Cracker Barrel to address and remedy the damage it did.

discomfort is temporary and, for most heterosexual people, it will pass with a little time.

I can understand why some heterosexual people might feel uncomfortable at the thought or sight of gay couples being affectionate with each other, even when the same behavior by heterosexuals would be deemed appropriate. If people haven't seen something before, the sight of it can startle and even frighten them. With increased exposure, for most people, it becomes a non-issue.

In the workshop I conduct, a little over half the participants indicate they would feel uncomfortable if gay colleagues did anything at a company picnic to indicate they and their significant others were a couple. The remaining participants say they are comfortable with gay people showing appropriate signs of affection. Those who say they would be comfortable generally are the ones who know gay people and have spent social time with them. Those who say they would be uncomfortable generally say they have not been with gay people socially. When the discussion is pursued, those who say they are comfortable acknowledge that the first time they saw two gay men or women hold hands it made them feel uneasy. But, they say, with time they felt at ease.

In my own life, I watched my family and friends grow to higher levels of comfort. Seeing gay men hug and kiss hello and good-bye was not something with which they were initially familiar. For many years, Ray and I refrained from displays of affection, even in our own home, when his or my family or heterosexual friends were present. Like most gay people I know, we tired of the "straitjacket" we had climbed into and began to dare, a little bit at a time, to be more honest and natural, particularly in our home.

I recall the first time we hugged in front of my folks. Ray was leaving for work. Mom and Dad were at the kitchen table having coffee. During their visits, we usually would walk to the front door and hug good-bye there to spare them any discomfort. But we had decided in advance of this visit not to change our daily routine. That day we would part company at the back door, as we normally did when no one was visiting.

That morning, everyone seemed to sense that something of significance was about to happen.

"Good-bye, Mac. Good-bye, Virginia," Ray said as he stood at the back door.

"Good-bye, Ray," they said as I made my way toward Ray.

"Good-bye, honey," I said as I approached him, my arms open preparing to hug.

And just as I was about to take Ray in my arms, my mother said to my father, "Mac, look at the cardinal in that tree over there."

Mom and Dad did what they needed to do at that moment in order to feel comfortable. They looked away. There was nothing wrong with that. Ray and I did what we needed to do, too. We hugged. On the second day of their visit, as I recall, Mom decided to take a quick peek. A day or so later, I was aware that Dad was glancing over, too. (We hugged for only a few seconds, so you had to look quickly.) With time, seeing their gay son hug his life partner, kiss him, and say good-bye became a non-issue for my parents. It became a non-issue for my 101-year-old grandmother, too. It is a non-issue for most of my siblings, nieces and nephews, aunts and uncles, cousins, neighbors, and friends.

With my family and friends, discomfort passed because there was an effort on my part to be myself and an effort on the part of those who love me to get past their initial anxiety. There was incentive: to have a closer network of family and friends.

The incentive in the workplace for getting over initial feelings of discomfort is having a closer network of colleagues. Gay, lesbian, and bisexual people who feel welcome to participate in all aspects of corporate life are more likely to feel valued and at home in the company. To ensure that happens, managers may need to go out of their way to be welcoming and to serve as positive role models for other employees.

My friend and colleague Mary Lee Tatum told of a gay attorney in Washington, D.C., who accepted a job in Arizona. He was so accustomed to being validated as a gay man by his Washington law firm that he assumed he and his male partner would be welcome at his new firm's holiday dance. They headed to the dance floor when the music was fast. Initially, they drew only curious glances. The music then turned slow. The male couple shrugged their shoulders and began to dance, at which point the dance floor emptied. They told Mary Lee that it felt like an eternity for them, but then former governor Bruce Babbitt and his wife joined them on the floor. Suddenly, couple after couple returned.

In this instance, the gay couple dared to participate fully in a corporate event. The former governor and his wife extended themselves and became role models for the others. Such a gesture of support is often necessary in an effort to create a welcoming work environment.

PUBLIC SUPPORT

The last item of concern is the need for public support from the company on the issues facing gay, lesbian, and bisexual workers. Often the opportunity arises for the company to give important witness to their commitment to their gay employees.

Using the analogy of the family again, gay men and women are always deeply moved by the sight of a person in a Gay Pride parade holding a sign that declares, "I'm proud of my gay child." My parents have been very generous in their contributions to the fight against AIDS. Like the sign in the parade, their donations serve as a reminder that they care about the issues that affect me. It makes me feel valued.

Gay, lesbian, and bisexual workers also look for signs of

support from their employers. This support can be shown by corporate sponsorship of AIDS fund-raisers. It is exciting to see people walking to raise money beneath a corporate banner. It can come in the form of commercial support of pro-gay television programming. Networks today are cautiously introducing minor gay characters to some television shows. In response, commercial sponsors of those programs have become the targets of campaigns by extremist groups who don't want any positive images of gay people presented. Maintaining commercial support of such programming is an important way to remind gay employees that the company cares about the issues that affect them.

Gay people throughout the country, likewise, appreciated the strong position of Levi Strauss and Wells Fargo Bank to deny requests for corporate donations from organizations that discriminate against gay people, such as the Boy Scouts of America. When AT&T was the target of a major letter and telephone campaign of protest against company support for Gay and Lesbian Awareness Week, management responded by stating they value all of their employees.

These concrete examples send clear messages to gay, lesbian, and bisexual employees and customers that the company means what it says when it officially lends it support. As AT&T Chairman Bob Allen underscored in "Our Common Bond," his statement on quality management, "We treat each other with respect and dignity, valuing individual and cultural differences."

Another example of giving witness to the seriousness of gay, lesbian, and bisexual issues is the corporate response to statewide referendums that seek to eliminate employment security for gay people. In 1992, the majority of voters in Colorado passed an amendment that prohibited the protection of basic civil rights for gay people at any level in the state. I was in Denver to conduct a couple of workshops shortly before the vote was taken and I found the atmosphere in the workplace intense and oppressive. Sponsors of the measure had filled the airwaves and mailboxes with horrible inaccuracies and wild accusations about gay people. Outrageous statements were repeated by a handful of employees in my workshop on homophobia. I was glad to get on an airplane for home, for I would not have wanted to work on a daily basis in that atmosphere.

I was very impressed, however, that into this emotional conflict stepped Apple Computer, Microsoft Corporation, U.S. West Communications, and Philip Morris Companies, among others, who wrote letters and/or contributed money for the defeat of the anti-gay measure. The bold actions taken by these companies were noticed and appreciated by gay and lesbian employees throughout the country and also by justice-oriented customers.

"Employment discrimination based on an individual's orientation is unjust," wrote Apple Vice President David Barram. "It also wastes vitally needed talent. We have a strong commitment, as a company, to encourage diversity in our work force. Besides the human dignity and fairness of that policy, we know it is important for our future success. Initiatives, such as Amendment Number Two, are not in the best interest of sound business."[6]

Particularly at this time, when some people seek to make the morality of homosexual behavior an issue of public debate and to abridge the rights of governments and corporations to protect gay, lesbian, and bisexual people from discrimination in employment, companies have a great opportunity to speak up for fairness. Silence in such situations is deafening. Providing a strong sign of support, on the other hand, communicates not only to gay employees but to all employees that diversity is a truly valued asset.

NOTE ON MARRIAGE

On May 5, 1993, the Hawaii Supreme Court, in a landmark decision, ruled that denying marriage licenses to same-sex couples violates the state constitutional guarantee of equal protection. The court ordered the state to either present "compelling" reasons for discriminating or to end its discriminatory policy. The ruling appears to open the door to same-sex marriage, although further litigation may be necessary to assure recognition of these marriages by other states and the federal government.

7 / Common Questions

IN THE COURSE of my work, some questions are raised so frequently that I feel they call for special attention in this book. Supervisors and colleagues of gay, lesbian, and bisexual employees often want to know:

"What are the AIDS-related issues we need to address and how can we be more supportive of our employees who are HIV-positive or who have AIDS?"

AIDS presents both challenges and opportunities to managers of the workplace today. Before we address how companies can be more supportive of all employees concerned about or affected by AIDS, let's take a quick look at what we know about the disease.

It is estimated by the Centers for Disease Control and Prevention (CDC) that approximately one to one and a half million Americans are infected with HIV (Human Immuno-deficiency Virus). About 50,000 more Americans are infected every year through: (1) unprotected anal, vaginal, and oral sex with an infected person; (2) sharing drug needles and syringes with an infected person; and (3) birth by an infected mother. Since the test for HIV antibodies was developed in 1985, the risk of HIV infection from a blood transfusion with infected blood or a transplant with infected organs or tissue is minute.

HIV attacks the body's immune system and reduces a person's ability to fight infections and disease. The result of the HIV infection is usually the development of AIDS (Acquired Immunodeficiency Syndrome).

The majority of the people infected with HIV: (1) are between the ages of twenty and forty-five; (2) are currently employed; (3) don't know they are infected; (4) won't show any symptoms of the disease for many years after infection; and (5) are living and working longer than those infected in the past, because of advances in medical knowledge and treatments.[1]

While there is no risk to co-workers or to the public from everyday interactions with an HIV-infected person, many people in the workplace have fears of and questions about AIDS. Even individuals who are well-educated about the transmission of the virus have concerns about the various ways HIV and AIDS can impact the workplace.

In response to these concerns, the National Leadership Coalition on AIDS, with a grant from the CDC, created guidelines for businesses in their response to AIDS. These guidelines were the basis of work by a coalition of business leaders, AIDS specialists, and others who created the New England Workplace Response to AIDS. The following ten principles have been widely circulated and strongly endorsed by businesses throughout the country.

1. Persons with HIV infection, including AIDS, in our company have the same rights, responsibilities, and opportunities as others with serious illnesses or disabilities.
2. Our employment policies comply with federal, state, and local laws.
3. Our employment policies are based on the scientific facts that persons with HIV infection, including AIDS, do not cause risk to others in the workplace through ordinary workplace contact.
4. Our management and employment leaders endorse a non-discrimination policy.

5. Specific training and equipment will be used when necessary, such as in health-care settings, to minimize risks to employees.
6. We will ensure that AIDS education is provided to all of our employees.
7. We will endeavor to ensure that education takes place before AIDS-related incidents occur in our workplace.
8. Confidentiality of persons with HIV infection and AIDS will be protected.
9. We will not screen for HIV as part of our pre-employment or workplace physical examinations.
10. We will support these policies through clear communication to all current and prospective employees.

Employing field-tested guidelines for responding to HIV and AIDS makes good business sense. These principles have helped both large and small companies prepare to address the many work-related issues raised by HIV and AIDS, such as:

- legal implications
- insurance costs
- disability requirements
- productivity
- employee morale
- customer concerns
- confidentiality
- discrimination concerns
- work disruption
- job accommodation

One of the most important steps a company can take to address HIV and AIDS is to educate all levels of the work force. In my workshops on homophobia, I have learned that most employees feel poorly informed about AIDS, particularly on the risks involved in sharing equipment such as a telephone or computer or sharing an office with an HIV-positive individual. Most employees also want more information on how best to be supportive of a person who is HIV-positive.

Education about HIV and AIDS should communicate clearly:

1. the company's policies concerning HIV and AIDS;
2. the ways HIV is and is not transmitted;
3. the legal rights of employees who are HIV-positive or have AIDS, particularly their right to confidentiality;
4. resources available to employees with HIV and AIDS and to their families;
5. how to respond to co-workers infected with HIV and to their family members;
6. how to prevent the spread of AIDS;
7. where to go for further, confidential information.

Effective AIDS education in the workplace may involve: providing reading materials to be taken home; inviting a person dealing personally with HIV or AIDS to speak to employees; showing a videotape on AIDS, followed by open discussion; inviting a health-care professional who specializes in HIV issues to speak to employees. There is an abundance of materials available to help companies design and implement successful training on HIV and AIDS. (For resources, see Appendix A.)

As with education about homophobia, leadership from management is essential for success. All levels of management should not only participate in training, but also strongly support it for their employees.

Legally, people who are HIV-positive or who have AIDS are protected by the Americans with Disabilities Act (1990), which prohibits discrimination by public- and private-sector employers based on actual or perceived disability. Companies that receive federal funds must also comply with the non-discrimination provisions of the Federal Rehabilitation Act. State and local laws that prohibit discrimination against people with disabilities are generally interpreted to protect people with HIV and AIDS, too.

These laws require employers to make reasonable accommodations to enable HIV-positive employees and those who have AIDS to continue working. This includes providing flexible work schedules, equitable leave policies, reassignment, and part-time work. Other laws of concern to companies with regard to AIDS and HIV are those pertaining to confidentiality and testing. It is important to be familiar with such laws and with current interpretations by the courts.

With thoughtful planning and education, employers are better able to respond with intelligence, fairness, and compassion to the issues raised by AIDS. By adopting the suggested principles to guide their response, companies can minimize the negative impact of AIDS on the workplace and build an even more productive and cohesive work force.

"How do you respond to the concerns of some people from religiously conservative backgrounds that the company's efforts on behalf of gay employees are endorsing a sinful lifestyle and that such efforts compromise the values of these employees?"

Coming from a strong religious background myself, I can empathize with the discomfort that some religiously conservative employees feel with the topic of homosexuality. My experience in the workplace has been that, though today's work force is multi-cultural and multi-religious, the most vocal response to this subject has been from individuals who identify themselves as Born Again or as fundamentalist Christians. Often in workshops, these employees will say, "As a Christian, I believe that homosexuality is a sin."

I gently remind these employees that it would be more accurate for them to say, "As a fundamentalist Christian, I believe homosexual behavior is a sin." Several heads in the audience nod approvingly as I point out that there are many people who identify themselves as Christian—Roman Catholics, Episcopalians, Methodists, Presbyterians, Southern Baptists, American Baptists, Congregationalists, to name only a few—and these Christians often have a wide range of beliefs about the morality of any number of issues, including divorce, birth control, abortion, alcohol consumption, and homosexual behavior. There are well-respected Scripture scholars in nearly every mainline denomination who believe that homosexual behavior is morally neutral and who argue that the Bible does not speak clearly about the subject. (In my own tradition, the Catholic Theological Society of America's Committee on Sexuality took such a position in their book *Human Sexuality: New Directions in American Catholic Thought.*)[2]

As previously stated, most people agree that the workplace ought to be free of religious pronouncements. While people may believe whatever they wish, expressing such thoughts will serve only to alienate and divide the work force. One can imagine the effect on productivity and on the company's ability to attract and retain the best and the brightest employees if the workday dialogue was peppered with such comments as "The Bible says divorce is a sin," or "I believe Jews are going to hell because they have not accepted Jesus as our Lord."

The vast majority of fundamentalist Christians I have met acknowledge the inappropriateness of making such comments in the workplace, but a few outspoken people have a difficult time separating workplace issues from their personal values and beliefs. One such person, a young man frustrated by the positive response his colleagues were giving my presentation, pleaded in a recent workshop, "I don't care what the company policy says. The future of civilization is at stake. Don't you understand that this is about the destruction of the Judaeo-Christian ethic?" Agitated beyond what seemed reasonable for the occasion, the young engineer then insisted, "I think we need to hear the other side."

Though I knew what he meant, I asked, "Do you mean we should have someone argue that homophobia is good for business?"

He scowled.

What this irate employee, who identified himself as a

Born Again Christian, wanted was a presentation to his colleagues on the inerrancy of the Bible and a reading of Genesis 19:4–11, Leviticus 18:22 and 20:13, 1 Corinthians 6:9–10, 1 Timothy 1:9–10, and Romans 1:26–27. These are the scriptural passages most often cited by those who believe homosexual behavior is a sin.

I don't raise the biblical issues in my corporate work because I believe that morality is a personal issue. But I do respond to questions, like the one I received not long ago from a public-relations employee who begged for help in understanding "why some religious people feel so strongly about the issue of homosexuality."

I cited the various relevant scriptural passages, explained the traditional interpretations, provided the interpretations of some contemporary theologians, and then offered insight on how well-meaning people can interpret the Scriptures so differently.

Some people believe that every word of the Bible was written by God and must be studied by every generation as strict guidelines for all human behavior. Other people, equally devout in their beliefs, hold that God inspired the writers of the Bible and that such revelation continues today. These people believe that the writers of the Bible were often caught in a cultural context different than the one we find ourselves in today. For instance, St. Paul's admonition that women should sit silently away from the men in temple so as not to distract them has been rejected by many people today who see it not as God's will but rather a reflection of a cultural bias about the status of women. There are a great many such examples.

Likewise, some devout Christians believe the Bible condemns homosexual behavior. At the time the Bible was written, people thought of homosexual behavior as a deviant, and sometimes hostile, act engaged in by heterosexual people. It has been only in the last century that social scientists began to understand homosexual orientation as an entity distinct from behavior and to see homosexual people as very different from heterosexual people in lifelong feelings of attraction. For that reason, many devout Christians believe the Bible's references to same-sex behavior reflect the cultural bias of the time and not God's will.

Another reason some religious people express such strong feelings is that they feel called to regularly "witness" their beliefs. This means that their commitment to their understanding of God takes precedence over all secular matters and they have the moral responsibility to share their beliefs with all others at every opportunity. Preachers who stand on the sidewalk and loudly read the Bible are witnessing. The people at televised sporting events who hold up signs in front of the cameras reading "John 3:16" are also witnessing. They want every viewer to be "born again in Jesus Christ." The irate young man in my workshop was also witnessing. He was speaking up for his beliefs.

The question this raises for employers is whether it is appropriate to witness one's personal values and beliefs in the workplace. If such witnessing is deemed non-disruptive by management, what guidelines will the company offer for "appropriate" statements of religious belief? In my workshop, I encourage people to speak up and express their feelings, but I ask them to use language that respects the feelings of others in the room. When the young man witnessed his beliefs by saying, "I think this is sick and disgusting and that homosexuality is a sin," he went too far. Such witnessing is destructive and completely inappropriate. It unsettles people and distracts employees from the work at hand.

You may have noticed that when the statement was made, "As a Christian, I believe homosexuality is a sin," I challenged not only the broad use of the word *Christian*, but also the imprecise use of the word *homosexuality*. It is not homosexuality that some people feel is sinful but rather *homosexual behavior*. The distinction is very important.

The leader of the successful 1992 effort to rescind and prohibit basic civil rights for gay people in Colorado said on television that people should not have job protection for something they did in their bedroom the night before. The strategy here is to try to reduce the issue of gay civil rights to a matter of behavior. But homosexuality is not a behavior any more than Judaism is a behavior.

Those religious denominations that believe homosexual behavior is morally wrong acknowledge that it is not being gay that is "sinful" but rather acting on one's feelings. I have often heard, "We love the sinner but hate the sin." Yet, as we discussed in Chapter Three, if I never again have sex in my life, I will still be a homosexual person. It is my inner feelings of attraction that make me so. And if I never have sex again but am fired from my job in Colorado or at the Cracker Barrel Restaurant chain because someone saw me march in a Gay Pride parade or testify against a gay basher in court, I am being fired not because of what I did in my bedroom the night before but because of who I am. A Jew does not have to go to temple in order to be Jewish, and anti-Semitism is not a reaction to Jews going to temple. When a company prohibits discrimination against Jews it does not care whether or not they go to temple or even if they privately celebrate Christmas. Nor does the company allow in the workplace witnessing about the "immorality" of Judaism. Nor does the company "present the other side" at workshops on anti-Semitism.

If employees complain that the company is endorsing an unacceptable lifestyle when it addresses gay, lesbian, and bisexual issues, I urge the company to respond firmly that moral positions on homosexuality are personal and should not be expressed in the workplace. If individuals insist that the company's efforts to create a safe work environment for gay employees "discriminates" against the religiously conservative employee and their values, I would ask them to: (1) utilize the support services, such as counseling, made available to distressed employees; (2) speak to their supervisors so that they will be aware of their stress; and (3) do their best to stay focused on the purpose of their time at work. If the stress is so great that they are unable to function at work, I would reaffirm the company's policy on discrimination and tell them if they could not be comfortable with this policy I would understand why they would feel it necessary to seek employment elsewhere.

Businesses have certainly had to deal with such conflicts in the past. There have been white employees who have felt compromised because they were "forced" to work with blacks, men who have felt oppressed by the presence of women, and members of one religious group upset because they have to "sit side by side" with members of another religious group.

In one of my favorite television programs, "I'll Fly Away," the wrestling coach sees his all-white high school team fall apart when he recruits a talented black student. A white young man quits the team in protest, expecting his coach to back down. The coach doesn't. One of the other white students in this Southern town in the 1950s confronts his father with the dilemma. "It isn't fair," he says in frustration. "You never had to deal with something like this." "No," says his wise father, "but this is a different time."

This is a different time, too. Today the issue at hand is homosexuality and the rights of gay, lesbian, and bisexual employees to work in a safe environment and to be treated as respectfully as any other employee.

"You use the term lover *here in Chapter Four," my eighty-year-old Dad said in reading my unfinished manuscript for this book. "That word brings up a lot of uncomfortable feelings for heterosexuals. You better change it."*

Words certainly can bring up uncomfortable feelings. Dad feels some people will wince when they read *lover*. I understand. I wince at words, too. For instance, as a gay man, I don't much like the word *faggot*, and I am struggling to become comfortable with the recent emergence in the gay and lesbian community of the word *queer* as socially acceptable.

Lover is a word I use with gay, lesbian, and bisexual people to describe my partner. Many gay people I know use the word *lover* for their significant other. It is a great word if you think of love as more than sex. Ray is the person I love and by whom I am loved.

But Dad is right and I don't generally use the word *lover* with heterosexual people because many heterosexual men and women think of the word as a sexual liaison outside of one's marriage. Because I am dedicated to the long, slow process of education about homosexuality, I generally try to use words that enable people to focus on what I believe are the important aspects of my message. Thus, with heterosexual people, particularly those I do not know well, I use the word *partner* to avoid reinforcing a stereotype. Although I know many gay, lesbian, and bisexual people use this word both privately and publicly to describe their significant others, I am not crazy about it because it feels devoid of the personal. Ebenezer Scrooge and Jacob Marley were partners.

I often get questions about language from workshop participants. Most people want to learn appropriate language because they don't want to feel awkward talking with gay, lesbian, and bisexual people. There is a fear of saying the wrong thing. I understand that anxiety. Actually, though, there's not a lot in gay vocabulary that is different from heterosexual vocabulary. *Love* means the same to both groups. So does *home, friend,* and *death.*

There are some words, though, that heterosexual coworkers might find it helpful to better understand. They are:

Homosexual—This word was created in 1869. Prior to that time, homosexual people were often referred to as *inverts.*

Webster's New World dictionary defines *homosexual* as "sexual desire for those of the same sex as oneself." The word can be used as a noun or adjective.

I often use the word *homosexual* when referring generally to people who feel sexual attraction for members of their own sex, but I make a distinction in my mind between a person who is "homosexual" and a person who is "gay." The word *homosexual* feels clinical. The word *gay* suggests to me a homosexual person with self-esteem. Likewise, I feel there is a formality to the word *homosexual*. When a person refers to me as a "homosexual," it feels as if they are calling me "Mr. McNaught." When a person refers to me as "gay," it feels like they are calling me "Brian." I like that.

Gay and lesbian people generally don't use the word *homosexual* in everyday language. But we don't all use the word *gay*, either. What words we use to describe ourselves and other homosexuals often depends upon with whom we are speaking and about whom we are speaking. The words we use to describe ourselves also can depend upon our age, our gender, out ethnic background, our politics, and even our HIV status.

Gay—This word, according to some historians, predates by several hundred years the word *homosexual* as a reference to people like me.[3] It did not come into popular usage as a description of homosexual people until the early 1970s. No one knows for sure why the word *gay* was selected, but it is today the word of choice and in all probability will remain so. I believe the word is best used as an adjective because it underscores that my sexual orientation is an aspect, not the totality of my being. I refer to myself as a gay man. (I feel the same about the words *lesbian, bisexual, homosexual,* and *heterosexual.*)

I know that it troubles some heterosexual people that the popular use of the word *gay* today means a homosexual person. Some men and women smile and nod in recognition when I say to an audience, "There are people who now feel very uncomfortable when singing old lyrics like, 'Don we now our gay apparel' or 'When Irish hearts are happy, all the world is bright and gay.'"

I like the word *gay*. I feel it is positive and, given its other meaning—joyous and lively, merry, happy, lighthearted—it truly reflects the seventeen years of my life with Ray.

I recommend the word *gay* for use in the workplace. It can be used for both men and for women, but *lesbian* is a better word to use when referring to gay women.

Lesbian—Long before Plato, Socrates, and Aristotle, a woman poet and teacher by the name of Sappho was honored by Greek society. She was a homosexual woman who lived with other women on the Greek isle Lesbos. From this the word *lesbian* was derived.

While homosexual women generally are not uncomfortable being referred to as gay, most prefer the word *lesbian*. For them, the word *gay* feels generic, whereas *lesbian* suggests a homosexual woman with self-esteem.

Use of this word underscores that homosexual women often have different priorities and experiences than gay men. Sexism prompts people to diminish the uniqueness of lesbian women. Studies, for instance, on the origins of homosexuality are almost always conducted by male researchers with male samples. Conclusions are erroneously generalized to include women or, just as bad, women are not even mentioned.

Often lesbian women have as much, if not more, in common with heterosexual women as they do with gay men. Lesbians share oppression with gay men because of homophobia and heterosexism, but they share oppression with other women because of misogyny and sexism. They also share health-care and productive concerns with heterosexual women. The use of the word *lesbian* acknowledges that the people we are describing are both gay and women.

Bisexual—Just as I have learned to incorporate the word *lesbian* into my language, I am working diligently to also include the word *bisexual*.

Bisexual people have the potential to feel erotic attractions for both genders. Bisexual men and women may or may not act upon those attractions. Whether they do or they don't, they are still bisexual in their sexual orientation. No one knows for sure how many people have a bisexual orientation. Many social scientists believe that bisexual attractions are the norm. Statistically, we know there are more people who engage in bisexual behavior than in exclusive homosexual behavior.

Although some bisexual people are equally attracted sexually to men and to women, most seem to have a preference, or what I refer to as a "major" and a "minor." Women are more likely to identify themselves as bisexual than are men. Perhaps this is the result of gender-role socialization or, as some researchers have suggested, right-brain–left-brain influences that enable women to be more comfortable with the flexibility associated with bisexuality.

Bisexual people often identify themselves as gay or lesbian because it affords them instant entree into the homosexual community. Also, these labels are better understood by all people than the label *bisexual.* Yet, bisexual people have different issues of concern than heterosexual or homosexual people. For instance, bisexual men and women who are heterosexually married can pass as straight but often don't emotionally relate to heterosexual people. Generally they identify with the oppression of gay and lesbian people because homophobia and heterosexism affect their lives, too. On the other hand, bisexual men and women who are in homosexual relationships may not completely identify with gay and lesbian people. Bisexual people are often poorly understood or unaccepted by both homosexual and heterosexual people alike. They are assumed to be gay and thought to be frightened of the label.

I recommend including the word *bisexual* in the workplace when referring to issues affecting gay, lesbian, and bisexual employees. Doing so communicates to bisexual men and women that there is an understanding that they too are affected by homophobia and heterosexism and that they have unique identities and needs.

Faggot—The source of the term *faggot* as a negative word for homosexual men may come from the days when the law called for such people to be burned at the stake. The word *fagot* was commonly used to refer to a bundle of sticks; one would throw the fagot on the fire. The practice of burning homosexual men and women to death may also be the source of the expressions *a flaming faggot* or a *flamer.*

Heterosexual people may overhear gay, lesbian, and bisexual people use the word *faggot* among themselves. Sometimes the word is used playfully and lovingly and sometimes bitterly. I have some serious reservations about the wisdom of minority people using the words of their oppressors in any manner. Our language generally betrays our bias and I fear that words like *faggot* and *dyke* reinforce negative stereotypes. I believe this is particularly dangerous for homosexual men and women in the early stages of developing self-esteem.

It should go without saying that it would be inappropriate to use the word *faggot* in the workplace. Gay people who use this and other prejorative words in the presence of heterosexual colleagues should understand that such behavior only confuses people who are looking for guidelines on what language is friendly and supportive.

Dyke—In her book, *Another Mother Tongue: Gay Words, Gay Worlds,* Judy Grahn suggests that the word *dyke* may have been derived from Dike of Greece, who was a storm goddess. As possibly a shortened version of *bulldyke,* the word may also come from Boudica, Celtic queen of the Iceni, who led her people in a revolt against the Romans in A.D. 61.[4] Whatever the source, the words *bulldyke* and *dyke* create images of masculine women. For many lesbian women, the word *dyke* is a powerful, self-affirming label. For others, the word remains a powerful put-down.

Heterosexuals, even those who feel they are trusted friends of the gay community, are best advised not to use the word *dyke* in reference to lesbians.

Queer—In the last few years, the word *queer* has been adopted by many gay, lesbian, bisexual, and transgender people (transsexuals and transvestites) as a strong, all-inclusive, confrontational, political label for sexual minorities. It's use purposefully underscores and celebrates the dictionary definition of *queer* as "differing from what is usual or ordinary; odd; singular; strange."

When gay people identify themselves as *queer*, they are generally attempting, like other minority groups, to defuse a hostile label and to boldly throw it back in the face of the oppressor as a challenge. Though heterosexual people are increasingly likely to hear or see this word as a self-identifying label, they should understand that its use is still considered offensive and inappropriate by many gay, lesbian, and bisexual people.

HIV—AIDS and HIV touch the lives of nearly every gay man and woman. Though lesbian women have the lowest risk factor in the world for contracting AIDS and other sexually transmitted diseases, and though most gay men will remain HIV-negative, AIDS is a constant uninvited presence in our lives. We have cared for and buried dear friends and lovers in numbers beyond what is comprehensible for people of any age. At holiday parties, we may find ourselves looking around the room and wondering who among our friends will be with us in a year. Such fear and loss can create enormous feelings of anger, frustration, fatigue, isolation, and resentment. It can also create an incredible sense of purpose, strength, and commitment. AIDS has both devastated the gay community and helped forge a new and powerful gay identity.

Heterosexual people who seek to better understand the wants and needs of gay, lesbian, and bisexual people must understand the immense influence of HIV and AIDS in our lives. Whether or not we are HIV infected, most gay people feel we are in a war that initially we were forced to fight alone. The militance that some people see in the gay community is a response to our long, painful war against AIDS, as well as our war with those who verbally and physically bash homosexual men and women. Both HIV and anti-gay bashings are at epidemic proportions today.

Gay Pride—Every year during the month of June, gay, lesbian, and bisexual people and heterosexual allies across the country celebrate gay pride to commemorate the Stonewall Rebellion, considered the birth of the modern American gay civil-rights movement. In large urban areas, parades attract thousands of men and women who march with bands, floats, and banners. In smaller towns, community picnics are organized and religious services are held as a way of participating in the celebration. In businesses across the country, gay, lesbian, and bisexual employees and their heterosexual supporters, often in conjunction with the Diversity Management office, celebrate Gay Awareness Week (or Month) by offering lunch-hour speakers and other educational programs, creating informational bulletin board displays, and walking as a group in local gay community parades.

Though homosexual women and men began to organize politically before the Stonewall Rebellion and laid the foundation for future organizing, it was the electric charge from the riots outside a gay bar in New York City that ignited a national gay-pride movement.

On June 29, 1969, the police were making a routine raid on the Stonewall bar on Christopher Street in New York City. When the police raided gay bars, they generally arrested everyone in the bar, transported them to the police station, and booked them for "lewd and lascivious behavior." At the police station, the individual bar patrons, often heterosexually identified married men, would pay a fine for a lesser charge rather than risk that their name would appear in the newspaper. Fear of public exposure had in the past made homosexual men and women easy prey for bullies of every stripe. But this time, the Stonewall patrons refused to cooperate and resisted this arbitrary harassment. Eventually, bricks were thrown at the police, who barricaded themselves inside the building. News reports of the ensuing three-day riots spread rapidly and "Gay Power" became a new civil-rights cry throughout the United States.

The closet—In American jargon "the closet" has come to mean a place where people keep a secret about themselves. When people publicly reveal their secrets, they are said to have "come out of the closet." Homosexual and bisexual men and women who conceal their sexual orientation from others are said to be "in the closet." For many gay, lesbian, and bisexual people, the closet is an apt description of the place in which you live when you are unable to tell your secret. The image that comes to my mind is a dimly lit, often stale, confining space in which it can be very difficult to stretch, breathe, and grow.

How do I help someone tell me that he or she is gay? And what do I say when I'm told?

Not every gay man, lesbian woman, or bisexual person is able to or wants to come out of the closet at work. Some gay people, as well as many heterosexual people, are private about their personal lives because that is the way they have been raised. Others are in relationships with individuals who feel strongly about staying in the closet. Still others are afraid their careers would be negatively affected if even one person discovered their sexual orientation. Whatever the reason, a person's decision to stay in the closet should be respected.

On the other hand, most closeted gay people I know wish that they could come out at work, and they say they would if they felt it was safe. Enabling such a person to come out of the closet could be an incredible gift not only to the gay person, but also to colleagues and the company. Coming out at work can contribute to one's sense of self-esteem. Being able to talk about oneself with a manager or a fellow employee usually improves personal relationships and increases loyalty. And, as I have stated before, coming out at work can increase productivity because it eliminates the need to put energy into hiding.

Despite all of the pluses, an employee who wants to help a gay colleague come out must first engage in some introspection. Questions to ask yourself include: Why do I think the person should come out? Is it for his or her benefit or for mine? In other words, is it to help the gay employee feel safer and more relaxed or is it to satisfy my curiosity? Is it to develop a closer relationship and show genuine acceptance of the employee or is it to prove to myself that I am an approachable or compassionate person?

If the motivation is mere curiosity, it is best to leave well enough alone. If your motivation is not the well-being of the closeted gay person, your response to the coming out and the necessary day-to-day follow-up will probably be inadequate and perhaps even harmful.

If, however, there is a genuine desire to help gay, lesbian, or bisexual co-workers feel safer, more comfortable, and more productive at work, then the task is to create windows of opportunity for disclosure. Gay people are prone to self-disclose with those they trust to be supportive. They learn who is trustworthy by watching and listening to people's behaviors and words. The proactive and reactive measures outlined in Chapter Six are a good start. As you recall, they include objecting to and not laughing at anti-gay jokes; confronting heterosexism and homophobia; attending workshops and presentations on gay-related issues; displaying in offices a book on gay issues, a supportive news clipping, or such gay-positive symbols as a "Safe Place" magnet.

If we are successful in creating the opportunity for disclosure and a colleague shares with us that he or she is a homosexual or bisexual person, the next step is to appropriately respond. If we happen to be one of the first people taken into the gay person's confidence, the event is of major significance. The individual may feel anxious and in need of a strongly supportive response.

It is perfectly normal to feel awkward or even uncomfortable when a gay person comes out, especially if we have not encouraged the disclosure. Nevertheless, it is essential at this time to be particularly sensitive to the special needs of the gay, lesbian, or bisexual colleague who has come out. There are a variety of responses that are appropriate. One might say:

"Thank you for telling me. I'm honored that you felt you could trust me. Unless you tell me otherwise, I'll assume that this information is between us. I won't tell anyone else without your permission. Have you shared this information with anyone else? What has it been like for you to work at this company without people knowing you are gay? Is there anything that I can do to make your life here a little easier?"

Other supportive comments include:

"My best friend (or sister, son, mother, cousin) is gay, too. I'm so proud of her (or him)."

"Is there an important person in your life? Yes? Well, I want to meet them!"

"Can you recommend something that I can read? I have a lot of questions and would love to learn more."

Although it would be a little harder to hear, I would nevertheless appreciate the honesty and the sensitivity if a colleague said to me, "Thank you for telling me. I know that couldn't have been easy. My religion tells me that homosexual behavior is wrong, so I admit to feeling conflicted about what you have said. However, as you know, I really like and respect you and that won't change. I think discrimination against gay people is wrong. Let me know how I can help you at work."

Responses that are neither helpful nor friendly include:

"Oh, no. Not you!"

"I don't think it's relevant."

"I'll pray for you."

I recall clearly the responses of my friends at work when I told them I was a gay man. Though they didn't know it, I had just previously attempted to take my life because I found the closet I lived in so oppressive.

One by one I took my colleagues from the newspaper out

to lunch to tell them who I was. On Monday, the editor-in-chief and I sat for a half hour as I played with my food and worked up my nerve to tell him.

"I admire your courage," he said when I finally told him. "That must have been hard for you to say."

His response was so supportive that upon returning to the office, I asked the women's editor, "Would you like to go to lunch tomorrow?"

On Tuesday, it took me only ten minutes to build up the courage to say, "There's something I need to tell you, Margaret. I'm gay."

"I don't know much about that," she admitted, "but I love you."

Affirmed by her response, when we returned to the office I said to the news editor. "Would you like to go to lunch tomorrow?"

The warm, loving, supportive responses I received from each co-worker enabled me to come a little bit further out of my closet. I trusted that with them I was safe to be the real Brian. I felt hope. I felt energized. And I recall, even twenty years later, how joyful I was to be in their presence at work. At least, initially.

Regrettably, it was also at this time that I learned my first important lesson about fighting homophobia: Educating people about homosexuality is a long, slow process that requires more than just having them like someone they know to be gay. When people become confused and frightened, as happened with my colleagues when I publicly affirmed my homosexuality, old, familiar, destructive ways of thinking can take over.

The mood of my office and the response of my colleagues changed when I acknowledged to a reporter from another newspaper that I was a gay man. My newspaper immediately dropped my weekly column. In retrospect, I know that my friends at work were confused. They liked me, but they were uneducated about homosexuality and felt ill-equipped to respond to the emotional public debate that followed my coming out. Some of my colleagues grew silent at work. Others were openly hostile. Though their behavior hurt me terribly at the time, I understand now that most of them did the best they could with what little information was available to them.

How are transgenderism, transvestism, and transsexualism related to the subject of homosexuality, and are they workplace issues?

The majority of transgenderists, transvestites, and transsexuals are heterosexual in their orientation,[5] but they are frequently linked to homosexuality for two reasons: (1) they often seek support and a voice through the gay, lesbian, and bisexual community; and (2) the public generally lumps all the groups together because they are all seen as "sexual minorities."

Transgenderism, transvestism, and transsexualism, like other diversity issues, are relevant to the workplace because: (1) Transgenderists, transsexuals, and transvestites work among us. It is estimated that there are tens of thousands of transgenderists and transvestites and thousands of transsexuals in the United States. They undoubtedly work in every profession. (2) The stress they experience from fear of discovery affects their ability to produce at their highest level. (3) If they are open about themselves, there likely is some stress present for both them and their colleagues. This stress affects teamwork and productivity.

The brief explanation offered here is intended only as a discussion starter. I am by no means an authority on transgenderism, transvestism, or transsexualism, nor am I an authority on the relevant laws and work-related issues. Nevertheless, in my work, I have met many bright, talented, though often stressed transgenderists, transvestites, and transsexuals who are American corporate employees.

Transgenderists are people who receive pleasure from wearing the clothing of the other sex. With few exceptions, they are generally men who wear women's apparel, ranging from undergarments only to complete wardrobe. These men are most often heterosexually married.

When a person of one gender wears the clothing of the other, it is called "cross-dressing." Those individuals who cross-dress do so for a variety of reasons. For instance, some people cross-dress because they identify more with the other sex emotionally. Some do so because they find the clothing of the other gender more comfortable. For others, it creates for them a pleasurable erotic response. Some people cross-dress because they receive pleasure from fooling other people. Others do it as a political statement, confronting society's preconceived notions of what makes a man a man or a woman a woman. Some even do it "just for the fun of it." With regard to regularity, some people cross-dress every day, others once a year.

Transgenderists are people who cross-dress because it makes them feel more comfortable emotionally. There are a variety of theories about why some individuals feel emotional pleasure from cross-dressing, suggesting that there is no simple explanation. For some, their emotional identity with the other sex is so strong that it creates an intense internal drive to cross-dress as often as possible. For others, the desire to cross-dress is less of a ruling factor in their lives.

Transgenderists who, in my opinion, present the corporation with the most pressing need for a response are those people whose emotional health is affected by their inability to cross-dress on a daily basis in full attire. Those women and men who regularly wear the undergarments of the other gender are invisible and seemingly quite content with their anonymity. But cross-dressers for whom wearing "gender appropriate" clothing is stressful, who are most comfortable and most energized by wearing the complete attire of the other gender, are in need of consideration by corporate policymakers. An easy initial step would be to educate service providers and diversity managers to the issues. (Resources are suggested in Appendix A.)

Transvestites are persons who cross-dress for erotic pleasure and/or relaxation. Some researchers define a transvestite as an individual who sexually stimulates him- or herself with or by putting on the intimate apparel of the other sex. This activity generally takes place only at home. Other researchers use a broader definition of transvestite to include those persons who experience sexual pleasure from wearing any or all the apparel of the other sex. In either description, the factor that separates transvestites from other transgenderists is the sexual motivation for cross-dressing.

Transsexualism is also an issue that demands corporate sensitivity. A transsexual is a person whose core gender identity is of the other sex. It is estimated that there are as many female transsexuals as there are male. We also know that these men and women generally identify with the characteristics of the other sex as early as age five and have always felt at odds with their genital anatomy.

Some transsexuals change only their outer appearance to coincide with their inner sense of self. However, they neither seek nor get sexual excitement from cross-dressing. To the best of their ability, as often as is possible, they live their lives consistent with their core gender identity. This may include using the "appropriate" restroom.

Many transsexuals opt to have their bodies surgically and hormonally reconstructed to match their gender identity. To be accepted for surgery, they are usually required to live a year or more as the gender they seek to genitally reflect. During this time, they take hormones of the other sex (estrogen or testosterone). Sex reassignment (or "sex confirmation," as many transsexuals would prefer it to be called) is a long, expensive process. Upon completion, transsexuals then seek to have birth certificates, employment records, and all other official documents changed to reflect their reality.

No one knows for sure what factors create the transsexual phenomenon. Like sexual orientation, there are probably multiple co-factors, some genetic, some hormonal, and some environmental.

Many companies are unaware that they employ transsexuals. These individuals came to the company surgically reconstructed. Other companies are confronted with this issue after the employee is hired. In either circumstance, it is once again important to have management and human-resource employees prepared to respond to the needs of the transsexual for a safe work environment. They must also be prepared to respond to the concerns of the transsexual's colleagues. As with every issue of diversity, educational programs go a long way in alleviating anxiety caused by a lack of familiarity with a subject.

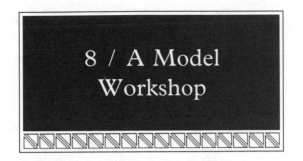

8 / A Model Workshop

"HELP! I JUST got a question I can't answer." The telephone-message request came from a gay employee about to lead his first in-house workshop for colleagues on the issue of homophobia in the workplace.

"We asked for questions in advance," he said. "One person cited a Masters and Johnson study and a Kinsey Institute study that allegedly reports you can change your orientation. I know you can't change, but how do I prove it? Did Masters and Johnson say that?"

No, they didn't. I recognized the quotes from a packet of materials assembled and distributed nationally by a group that opposes civil rights for gay people. Those same misrepresentations had popped up verbatim in my workshops from time to time. My advice to the gay employee was to acknowledge up front he was not a sexuality educator, to speak from his heart as a gay person, and to stay focused on workplace issues. He did so and called to say proudly that the workshop was a success.

I would like to have been there to help correct the misrepresentation of the Masters and Johnson study and of the Kinsey Institute research because such inaccuracies perpetuate ignorance. Providing accurate information helps create understanding and a tolerance of difference. But it isn't always possible or practical for a company to have present a trained homophobia educator. Nevertheless, companies themselves can design effective education about homophobia, particularly when the sessions involve input from gay, lesbian, and bisexual employees.

The suggestions offered here for designing and implementing a workshop on homophobia or on gay issues in the workplace are based upon my own work and reflect my bias about effective education.

Having a clear set of goals, I believe, is the most important first step. What is the company trying to accomplish and why? If the company is clear about why it is making the effort, it won't get sidetracked by non-issues, such as what the Bible does or doesn't say. This is of interest to some people but ultimately not essential to the discussion.

The company's overall goal for diversity training is generally the creation of a more productive work environment for all employees. More specifically, the company's goals for the workshop might be (1) establishing the company's commitment to non-discrimination against gay, lesbian, and bisexual employees; (2) providing information on the extent of homophobia and its impact on all employees; (3) building allies in the effort to eliminate homophobia. Having clear goals decreases the likelihood that confused employees will ask, "Why are we here? Is the company trying to dictate our moral beliefs?"

The stated goals for my workshop, formulated in collaboration with my corporate clients, are:

1. Employees will understand the corporate commitment to and policy on non-discrimination (where applicable).

    Sometimes employees are unaware that management has taken a formal stand on this issue. Learning of such a commitment is an important first step in securing the employees' openness to addressing gay issues in the workplace. If the company does not have a non-discrimination policy (see Chapter Six), an educational effort for policymakers would be a wise starting point.

2. Employees will explore and articulate thoughts and feelings on homophobia, heterosexism, and homosexuality.

This is the core issue of the workshop. Provided with a supportive atmosphere, participants need to be encouraged to ask questions and appropriately express feelings. (As previously stated, employees are asked to respect all views and avoid put-downs when they express themselves.) If education, and not merely dictating company policy, is the goal, it is essential to ensure that all questions and comments are welcome. I tell participants that I want them to feel free to raise their hands at any point to comment on what I have said. "If we disagree, we'll acknowledge that we have a difference of opinion and move on," I add.

There is a distinction between dialogue and debate. Dialogue is important to answering questions many people have. Debate bogs down the process, often bores the other participants, and takes valuable time away from other topics of concern. Offering to meet during the break or at the end of the workshop with anyone who wishes to further discuss an issue is a nice way of ending a protracted single-issue debate.

3. Employees will replace myths about homosexuality with accurate information.

As I have stated before, ignorance is the enemy. Lack of exposure to a subject such as homosexuality generally creates anxiety. Many people are misinformed about gay, lesbian, and bisexual people. Replacing myths ("Gay people choose to be gay") with accurate information ("People don't choose their sexual feelings, only whether or not they will act on them") helps lower anxiety. In the workshop, I provide the most current information about homosexuality, but I always encourage the participants to do their own reading on the topic.

Gay, lesbian, and bisexual speakers can also be very effective in dispelling common myths. Ideally, these speakers should be employees of the company.

4. Employees will explore the effects of homophobia on all employees.

Even people who hold strong negative beliefs about homosexuality are often shocked to discover the impact jokes and offensive comments have on their colleagues. Once fair-minded individuals fully understand the effects of homophobia, they are less inclined to tolerate inappropriate behaviors in the workplace.

5. Employees will strategize means of eliminating destructive behaviors from the workplace.

People can agree that inappropriate behaviors ought to be stopped but not know how to do it. My colleagues and I ask the participants, "What happens if you are at the lunchroom table and your office mate starts to tell an AIDS joke or makes an anti-gay comment? How do you step in? Is there a comfortable way to change the subject?"

What follows is a description of the workshop I conduct either alone or with a colleague. It is offered here as a model of effective training on gay issues in the workplace. Feel free to borrow, copy, revise, or ignore.

No two workshops I conduct are exactly the same. They are made different by the unique quality of each audience, by my variability, and by the variability of my co-facilitator. Any workshop will reflect the personality, experience, and priorities of the presenter(s) and participants.

That said, I believe it is important to have the workshop begin with a strong statement of support from a person in management. He or she can set the stage by underscoring how seriously they take the issue and how glad they are to provide this opportunity for everyone to explore the subject. If it is a department meeting, it ought to be the department head who introduces the workshop. If the workshop is sponsored by the company's diversity management office, a representative of that office should open the session by discussing the company's commitment to creating a safe, productive work environment.

Employees who feel anxious or confused about the subject often take their lead from their supervisors. Two examples of how managers can affect the atmosphere of a workshop on gay issues come quickly to mind.

The manager of one department showed up halfway through my workshop for his employees. No one introduced me or the topic to the group. I introduced myself and spent a considerable amount of time making the case for why this subject was a work-related issue. It was at this workshop that the angry engineer (referred to in Chapter Seven) pleaded with his colleagues, "I don't care what the company policy says. The future of civilization is at stake."

The manager of another department attended my workshop in advance of inviting me to speak to his group. He then called each of his employees and told them why he had invited me and why he wanted them to attend the workshop. On the day of the event, he introduced the subject by explaining his own understanding of how bias can take a terrible toll. As a high school student, he said, he was part of a gang of boys who taunted a young man who was gay. He explained how horrible he felt when the gay student committed suicide. He set the tone for our time together. His employees were serious, attentive, and asked sensitive questions about how productivity is affected by homophobia.

In my experience, management almost always sets the tone, for good or for bad.

I also believe strongly that there should be some gay or lesbian presence in the workshop. If the facilitator is a heterosexual person, gay, lesbian, and bisexual people should be brought in to talk about how homophobia and heterosexism have affected their lives. If there are not gay employees who are available or feel safe enough to speak to the group, most cities have gay speaker's bureaus. If that is impractical, there are audiovisual aids that can be used (see Appendix A).

Having gay people speak about their lives allows some heterosexual people their first opportunity to put into perspective all they have heard about homosexual men and women. Providing a human being who challenges the myths, the jokes, and snide comments is a very effective means of raising awareness. More than any facts I offer, my presence as a happy, self-affirmed gay man is the most powerful tool I have to combat ignorance on this issue. In this instance, the messenger becomes the message.

When I arrange for gay and lesbian guest speakers, I always request a man and a woman. If only one can come, I ask that it be a lesbian woman so that the audience doesn't see and hear the issue from only my perspective as a white male.

My co-facilitator is most often my friend Pamela Wilson. In addition to being a nationally known, highly skilled sexuality educator and trainer, author, and editor, she is an African-American, heterosexual woman. I love the black-white, female-male, straight-gay balance our collaboration provides. Such diversity allows a great number of participants to connect or identify with our life experiences and perspectives.

Following the introduction by the department head or representative of the diversity management office, I present the goals of the workshop and the premises of our time together. It is here that I outline (as in Chapter One) how homosexuality, homophobia, and heterosexism are work-related issues.

The premises, again, are:

1. The corporation is making an effort to create a safe, productive work environment for all employees.
2. Gay people and people who care about them work among you.
3. Heterosexism and homophobia are present in the workplace, manifested in negative comments, jokes, or assumptions of heterosexuality (heterosexism).
4. Homophobia and heterosexism take a toll on people's ability to be productive in the workplace.
5. Homophobic behavior results from misinformation, fear, and a lack of exposure to gay people. Education reduces

the chance that people will engage in or tolerate homophobic behavior.

6. Employees are entitled to their own belief systems. Tolerance does not equal acceptance. It is inappropriate behavior, not beliefs or values, we seek to change.

While stating and building a strong case for each premise,
I attempt to learn more about the audience. I will ask, for
instance, how many people, by show of hands, know someone who is gay. Usually, at least half to three-quarters of the
participants raise their hands, depending upon where in the
country the workshop is taking place. The geographical location also influences the response when I inquire, "How
many of you know someone who is HIV-positive?"

When building the case for the effect of ignorance on the
anxiety we feel over this issue, I report George Gallup's findings that only 15 percent of Americans feel they had good sex
education at home and only 10 percent had good sex education in high school. Again, I ask group members to raise
their hands if they believe they received good sexuality education at home or school. Typically, only one or two people
put their hands up, indicating their parents did a decent job
of talking to them about sex. Likewise on the second question, I'll see only a few hands, and those raised hesitatingly,
to indicate that they had a good sex-education program in
high school.

"In our house, we didn't talk about sex," I offer. "And in
my all-boys Catholic high school, taught by the Christian
Brothers of Ireland, we got only a half-hour film from the
Navy on gonorrhea. Most people my age learned about sex
by laughing at jokes we didn't get. We would pretend we
understood but had to go home and try to figure it out for
ourselves. We didn't have Phil and Oprah to explain things
to us." People laugh and nod in recognition.

I also remind them, as I have previously observed in this
book, that none of us had books at home or in school that
explained homosexuality. "Where were we to look if we

wanted to find out about these people we called 'queer'?" I ask. "What was the source of our factual information about homosexuality? Given this, how can we be expected to be comfortable with something we've never had the chance to learn about or discuss?"

My style of education is very personal. I believe that in building one-to-one relationships, I can break through the "them versus us" mentality that often separates homosexual people from heterosexual people. My attitude toward my audience is that most of the men and women sitting in the room want to know more than they do. Most of the participants have had very little opportunity to ask questions about this issue. Most feel anxiety about the time we are going to spend together, and most are pretty nice people who don't want to feel fear. Many of them are now seeing a gay person up close for the first time. Most do not have strong religious beliefs on this issue, but some do. Most of them are used to being made to feel guilty about their racism, sexism, and anti-Semitism (among other prejudices) in "diversity" classes, and they expect that is my intent. I also believe that most of them need to feel safe, need to feel understood before they will be willing to share.

Pam is very good about establishing ground rules that help people feel safe. Before introducing the first exercise, which has as its goal surfacing the feelings of the participants, she reminds them that we are talking about two difficult issues: sexuality and difference. She also acknowledges how hard it can be to speak up in an environment of peers where you are expected to know and parrot company policy. "We are sometimes afraid of saying stupid things, aren't we?" she says. "Well, let's agree that the only stupid question is the one we don't ask. And let's agree that we will keep an open mind today. Sometimes we find ourselves disagreeing with a comment before someone finishes the sentence. Let's let everyone finish before we judge the comment. And let's avoid put-downs like 'Boy, is that dumb.' We're all here to learn and we're entitled to our feelings."

The first exercise we offer, referred to in the Introduction, is a "continuum choice" exercise. Four easels are generously spaced at the front of the room. A flip chart is on each. Pam poses three questions, one at a time, and in response to each, she asks the participants to stand in front of the flip chart that best answers the question from their perspective. We remind the participants there are no wrong answers.

Exercises such as this help us achieve the goal of providing the participants the opportunity to discuss and learn more about the issues. With the continuum choice exercise, any set of questions can be created. Ours are:

1. How would you describe the atmosphere for gay, lesbian, and bisexual employees in your workplace? Would you say it is very hostile, somewhat hostile, somewhat accepting, or very accepting?

2. If a new employee came to you and confided that he or she was gay, what would you think was the best thing for him or her to do, given your assessment of the workplace: stay in the closet, come out to only a few close friends, come out to a supervisor, or come out to everyone?

3. There is going to be an office picnic on Friday. Every employee is invited to bring family members. An openly gay employee plans to come. Would you be most comfortable if he or she would: come with a date of the other sex, come alone, come with a same-sex date but refrain from engaging in any displays of affection, or come with a same-sex date and feel as free as heterosexual co-workers do in engaging in displays of affection. (We explain here that we are talking about *appropriate* indications that the two are a couple.)

Once participants have placed themselves along the continuum, we ask a few volunteers to talk about why they chose to stand where they did. Lively discussion among the employees generally results from the exchange. We encourage participants to make up a fifth option if none of the options we provided suits them, or to feel free to move from easel to easel if they change their mind at any point during the discussion.

The value of beginning with such an exercise, time permitting, is that it ferments thought about the conditions of the office and about personal feelings. It also almost always guarantees that the myths that will later be addressed are raised by the participants themselves. These include: I don't tell my colleagues my personal business. Why do I need to know that someone is gay? If people choose a homosexual lifestyle, that's their business, but why is it a work-related issue? I wouldn't want them coming to the picnic with a date because I am afraid it would influence my children's development.

It's best for the facilitator not to argue with statements made by the participants in this exercise. The purpose of this segment is to get people to think and to express their thoughts and feelings. Often these thoughts and feelings are based upon misinformation. If Pam or I hear a myth, we interject, "Some people believe that. We'll talk more about that later."

Following this exercise, the program proceeds to an important presentation on sexuality. The introduction to this section includes the acknowledgment that scientists are still in the process of studying and understanding the full dimensions of human sexuality and that we have much more to learn. It also includes the encouragement that everyone read for themselves current literature on the subject.

Our presentation on human sexuality provides the important distinctions between biological sex, gender identity, gender role, and sexual orientation. Workshop participants also learn about Alfred Kinsey's research into American sexual behaviors and about how sexual orientation is different than sexual behavior and sexual orientation identity. (See Chapter Three for a more detailed presentation of this information. Please also see Appendix A.)

It is this section of the workshop that lays the important groundwork for understanding how homophobia is like racism and sexism. It is here that we address the issues that often make this topic most confusing for some people. Of particular importance to many of the participants is hearing that people don't choose their sexual orientation. The other distinction that helps clarify the issue for some people is that homosexuality is not defined by behavior but, rather, by feelings, whether or not those feelings are acted upon.

At this time, a facilitator should expect the most questions and the most debate. The questions often come from parents who want to learn more about the sexual development of their children. They appreciate the opportunity to clarify the issues of gender identity, gender role, and sexual orientation.

If there is debate, as sometimes happens, it often comes from people who feel that much of the information being presented is biased. These individuals will generally insist that homosexuals choose to be gay and can change their sexual orientation.

Pam and I have found that the factual information on sexuality and sexual orientation changes the way many people see these issues. Most participants are amazed by what they did not know. If disagreements arise from this factual presentation, facilitators should prevent debates by agreeing to disagree and moving on.

If it is not possible to offer in the workshop a component on sexuality, at the very least companies should provide written resources for the participants. These may include recommended readings and/or a list of the materials available in the company's library or human-resource office.

As I mentioned earlier, gay, lesbian, and bisexual employees should, if possible, be asked to participate in diversity workshops as speakers. This provides a wonderful opportunity for heterosexual co-workers to ask questions and to learn firsthand how homophobia and heterosexism can impact a person's life. In the process, some people will let go of old stereotypes and biases. Having a gay employee speak also provides the closeted homosexual person in the audience a positive role model. Watching the other members of the audience respond to the gay speaker with respect, and often with support, likewise presents the closeted employee with a vision of what is possible for him- or herself.

These gay, lesbian, and bisexual employees or volunteers from outside of the company should be provided sufficient time to talk about their lives and about their work. I believe that it is particularly helpful if the gay people offer enough personal information about themselves to enable a heterosexual colleague to connect person to person. An example might be:

"Hello. My name is Patrick Mooney. I'm thirty-eight years old. I've worked at this company for twelve years in the public-relations office. I'm the middle child of five Irish Catholics. I'm out to my parents and siblings and recently told my office mate that I am gay. I came out at work because I was tired of lying and hiding and I was sick of hearing AIDS and fag jokes. I've been in a relationship for eleven years. I have to admit to being a little nervous about being here because I see some people in the audience that I know but who didn't know that I am gay. I am going to stop talking now so that Kathleen can tell you about herself. But if you have any questions for me, I hope you'll feel comfortable asking."

Ample time should also be allowed for questions. It is here that heterosexual employees have the best opportunity to bridge the gaps that separate them from their gay colleagues. They can do so by asking for information that will help them better understand the issues. Appropriate questions include: How long have you known you were gay? How did your parents respond? How did your office mate respond? Does your boss know? Are you afraid that coming out at work will affect your career? Why do I need to know you are gay? How has coming out affected your attitude about work? What do you want from the company? How can I be supportive?

Questions that I would consider inappropriate would be those that seem hostile, too personal, or call for opinions the gay volunteer isn't qualified to offer. Examples of such questions would be: Do you believe you are living in sin? Have you tried to change? What do you do sexually? Do you have AIDS? Is the singer Madonna a bisexual?

I also think that gay, lesbian, and bisexual employees who volunteer to speak ought not to be expected to present the latest scientific research on the frequency of homosexuality among identical twins, to explain the Salk Institute study on brain differences in gay and heterosexual men, or to provide a thorough explanation of how domestic-partner benefits are set up in corporations like Levi Strauss. These men and women are experts in their particular professions. They also happen to be gay and have volunteered to talk about their lives. Being gay, lesbian, or bisexual, as they well know, doesn't make them an authority on homosexuality. They are best used as resources of how it feels to be a gay employee of the company. And what a great resource they are!

The next exercise we introduce helps the participants surface, discuss, and learn more about the myths about homosexuality. The employees are asked to provide us with the words our culture uses to describe gay people. "Pretend you are all from another planet. We have sent you out with pen and paper to report on how homosexual people are perceived. Let's start with the names we have for homosexual men and women. Please just call them out and we will record them on the flip charts at the front of the room."

The words we get include *gay, lesbian, homosexual, he/she, fag, dyke, bulldagger, butch, homo, queer, queen, sissy, pansy, fairy, fruit, lezzie, punk, shim, mariposa,* and *poof,* among others.

"What images did you hear about?" we'll ask. "What mannerisms were discussed?"

We record *limp wrist, lisp, light in the loafers, swishy* (for men), and *manly* (for women).

Under "professions" we get *hair dresser* for men and *truck driver* for women, among others.

When we ask for any other words that come to mind, we hear *promiscuous, AIDS, child molesters, transvestite, transsexual.*

Once we have surfaced these words, I explain their origins and meanings (as I did in Chapter Seven). I challenge the myths by citing current studies, such as the ones that show that most sexual abuse of children involves a young girl with an adult male in her family. I also point out how all of the slang terms for gay men are feminine or "soft" words (*sissy, pansy, fairy*) and all of the slang terms for lesbian women are masculine or "hard" words (*butch, bulldagger, dyke*). This underscores how many people confuse homosexuality with gender role and gender identity. One of the myths about homosexuality is that gay boys and gay girls are confused about and uncomfortable with their gender.

It is also at this time that I offer my perspective on the close link between sexism, homophobia, and heterosexism. (See Chapter Three.)

The advantage of this popular exercise is that it surfaces the stereotypes people have of homosexuals and provides an opportunity to discuss the myths; it creates a snapshot of the world in which gay, lesbian, and bisexual people are forced to live; and it presents the case for appropriate use of language.

With the backdrop of these offensive words and images, I then dramatize the destructive power of homophobia by describing what it is like to grow up as a gay person. I do this in two ways. First, I lead the group through a "guided fantasy" that makes real the isolation and pain of having a secret you don't understand and are afraid to share with anyone for fear that they won't love or respect you anymore. Described in detail in Chapter Two, the role reversal helps heterosexual employees understand why a gay colleague might need to come out and to understand what the person means when he or she says, "I'm gay."

The other way I bring home the powerful negative impact of homophobia and heterosexism is by telling my story of growing up as a gay man. It is a sometimes humorous but generally painful description of fear, denial, struggle, despair, and ultimately self-acceptance and love. By the vote of nearly every post-workshop evaluation ever completed for my workshop, the telling of my story is the most powerful tool in communicating the seriousness of the issue of homophobia.

The truth is, it could be any gay person's story. What happens when homosexual men and women tell their story is that heterosexual people are able to imagine us as vulnerable children, confused and frightened by our feelings. It is then that they are best able to understand the difference between sexual orientation and sexual behavior. It is for that reason that I stress once again that these workshops must provide participants with the opportunity to meet and talk honestly with a self-affirmed gay man, lesbian woman, or bisexual person on a personal level.

The last exercise of our day-long workshop helps the employees strategize the means of eliminating destructive homophobic, heterosexist, and AIDSphobic behaviors from the workplace. We ask six people from the audience to participate in a scripted role play that depicts a conversation full of bias against homosexual employees.

The scenario has six employees sitting at the lunchroom table discussing the assignment of a new person to their work area.

PAT: Have you met the new guy who has been assigned to our area? He seems nice enough. Whose office is he going to share?

CAROL: He does seem nice enough, but there's a rumor flying around about him. Someone from his other location called to report that he's gay.

TERRY: You're kidding. Well, he's not going to share *my* office. I mean it. I'll quit first.

PAT: What are you so worked up about?

TERRY: Would you want to share an office with a fag? What if he has AIDS? What are people going to think of me? There's an opening in my office, but he's not going to be in it.

CAROL: Maybe he should work with Bill. Rumors fly about him, too. Have you ever seen him at an office function with a woman?

TERRY: That's a perfect solution. The new guy can work with Bill. That way we can confine the germs to one area. And who knows, maybe romance will bloom.

TED: I'm real uncomfortable with this conversation.

CAROL: Oh, come on, Ted. Terry has a right to his opinion.

Following the reading of the scenario, we ask the participants as a group, "Do you think this conversation could happen in your work environment?" Generally the answer is yes. We then ask the employees to break into groups of four and answer the following three questions:

1. How would you feel if you were a gay person sitting at that table, and how might it affect your work?
2. What examples of homophobia and heterosexism can you identify in the conversation?
3. What steps could you take to address the homophobia and heterosexism present in the conversation?

When the group reconvenes, we process their responses to questions 1 and 2 and record on flip charts their interventions for question 3. Their interventions are listed under two headings: *Reactive* and *Proactive*. The reactive measures that are often suggested include using humor to derail the conversation; refusing to laugh at anti-gay humor; educating colleagues about AIDS, heterosexist assumptions, and homosexuality; citing company policy about non-discrimination; pulling Terry aside to confront him with the effects of his behavior; leaving the table; reporting the conversation to a supervisor; personalizing the issue by saying, "I know gay people and I'm offended by this conversation"; or saying, "The new guy can share my office."

As we help the participants explore which response feels most comfortable for them, we also ask, "Is Carol correct? Does Terry have a right to express his opinion?" A lively, thoughtful discussion generally follows. Most people agree that if it is appropriate to express opinions on controversial topics at work, then a person should use non-inflammatory language. Even then, they say, they wish the company would provide clear guidelines on when, where, and if such discussions should take place.

Under the proactive heading, we list "personal" measures and "corporate" measures that can be taken in a preventive manner to create an environment that is free of homophobia. As described in more detail in Chapter Six, the personal measures include attending a workshop on homophobia in the workplace; displaying a pro-gay symbol or book in your office; talking positively to colleagues about the issue; and using inclusive language (*partner* rather than *spouse*). As also previously stated, the corporate measures include, among others, having a non-discrimination policy; offering training on the issue; providing domestic-partner benefits; and supporting gay employee groups.

At the end of our workshop, participants meet and interact with representatives of the company's gay, lesbian, and bisexual employee support group. These representatives, usually a woman and a man, sometimes a heterosexual and a homosexual person, talk briefly about themselves, their work, and why they are involved in the support group. They also explain the group's goals, provide resources, and explain how to participate in the group's activities. They then answer questions from the workshop participants.

Prior to leaving the workshop, employees are asked to fill out an evaluation. Each company provides its own form, but typical questions include:

Rating from 1 (Very Positive) to 5 (Very Negative)
1. In general, how do you feel about the workshop?
2. How meaningful was the workshop to you as a member of this company's working environment?
3. How meaningful was the meeting to you as an individual?
4. How would you rate the effectiveness of the consultants?
5. How would you rate the effectiveness of the workshop as a whole?
6. If you have attended other affirmative-action workshops, how did this session compare?

Providing the opportunity for feedback, the questions asked can include:

1. Which of the workshop's activities was most meaningful to you? Please explain why.
2. Did this workshop give you any new insights about your own attitudes? Please explain.
3. Do you have any additional comments or observations you would like to make?

Questions that target the subject more directly include:

Yes or No?
1. I know that the company's Affirmative Action/Equal Employment Opportunity policy covers sexual orientation.
2. I believe that homophobia is a problem in society.
3. I believe that homophobia is a problem in our company.
4. I believe that homophobia is an appropriate topic for an affirmative-action meeting.
5. I would take action if I witnessed homophobic behavior outside of work.
6. I would take action if I witnessed homophobic behavior at work.

The results of these post-workshop evaluations and questionnaires can assist the company enormously in determining the success of the training, in redesigning the training, and in assessing employee support.

In-house diversity trainers and gay and lesbian employee speakers have an abundance of resources available to them for designing and presenting workshops on gay issues in the workplace. These materials include books that explain current research on homosexuality and describe useful training exercises. Also available are audiovisual aids that effectively communicate the personal and professional dynamics of the issue. (For more information on these resources, see Appendix A.)

Epilogue: / From Here to Where?

As with fighting racism, sexism, and anti-Semitism, working to eliminate homophobia and heterosexism is a long, slow, demanding, sometimes frustrating, but always rewarding process. Rooting out bias based on fear is like pulling pervasive, aggressive weeds that choke the life out of blooming plants.

"This must be rewarding work for you," commented a woman who lingered after a recent workshop.

"It is," I said, "primarily because I know it touches people's lives." I feel privileged to be part of the effort.

Corporations who make the effort to create a safe and inclusive working environment for gay, lesbian, and bisexual people are doing more than helping "maximize productivity" or "attract and retain" the best and the brightest employees. They are also deeply touching people's lives.

Fighting homophobia and heterosexism in the workplace makes good business sense. Creating an even playing field for this 10 percent of the work force makes them more competitive and loyal employees. The non-discrimination policies that are implemented, the "homophobia" workshops that are offered, and the equitable benefits programs that are assembled make the workplace more professional. But these efforts also create a garden of human development where people cannot only "do their jobs," but can also grow into happier, healthier individuals.

It is, I believe, no small gift to society when the company creates an atmosphere in which its employees can learn to respect themselves and their neighbors. When the company teaches "tolerance," it not only ensures a more cohesive work force, but also gives to its employees what some people can't find anywhere else in society: an opportunity to be valued because of one's skills, regardless of race, creed, color, gender, national origin, physical ability, or sexual orientation. While I know that is not the primary purpose of business, it is certainly a worthwhile benefit.

When the company assesses the value of its efforts to ensure a safe and productive work environment for gay employees, I hope it puts into the "plus" column the names of the gay men, lesbian women, and bisexual people whose lives they have improved, the names of the families of gay people who have been mended or strengthened, and the names of the heterosexual men and women who are grateful for being freed to move beyond their fears of difference.

One Bellcore employee acknowledged the significance of his company's efforts on this issue when he wrote, "I realize that I will never fully comprehend just how difficult, frustrating and scary it must be for young homosexual people to grow up in a mostly heterosexual world, but, thanks to you, I now have been sensitized to the issues that they face in their day-to-day lives. I only hope that I can be one of the people who are willing to stand up and say 'enough already' when someone starts spouting an offensive joke or puts somebody down just because they're different than the majority."

Besides seeing profit as a sign of success, I hope companies also take pride in the way they create awareness and acceptance of human diversity.

I believe that in the not too distant future, if they don't already do so, companies who have addressed homophobia and heterosexism will look at their efforts with pride and satisfaction. While they can expect that some employees will want to continue debating personal beliefs about homosexual behavior, companies who make good-faith efforts can also expect that the fearful and hateful behaviors that currently cause divisiveness, fear, and dysfunction will be nearly eliminated.

I also believe that someday, maybe even in my lifetime, tolerance of difference in the workplace will turn into a true celebration of diversity. People's differences will be treasured as strengths. We will recognize that what makes each employee unique guarantees a company's competitive edge.

AT&T Chairman Bob Allen said as much when he addressed the National Coalition of 100 Black Women in 1991: "In my business we have some 270,000 people—people of all kinds. I want AT&T to be the kind of business where diversity is seen as an asset, not a threat . . . a business where we respect and honor our differences and respect and honor our common humanity, our common goals. I want AT&T to be a business where all people are free to dream . . . and free to pursue their dreams."

Someday, the full talent of gay, lesbian, and bisexual employees will be recognized, appreciated, and tapped by a majority of employers. Someday, the diversity represented in gay people will be seen as an asset, not a threat. Instead of debating whether gay people choose or can change their sexual orientation, society will celebrate the richness that gay, lesbian, and bisexual people bring to the table. It will be then that all employees will truly be "free to dream . . . and free to pursue their dreams."

Until then, we all have a lot of long, slow, demanding, sometimes frustrating, but always rewarding work ahead of us.

Appendix A

RESOURCES

The newsletters, organizations, books, videos, and brochures listed here are valuable resources for the ongoing work of creating a safe and productive environment for gay, lesbian, and bisexual employees.

NEWSLETTERS

Gay/Lesbian/Bisexual Corporate Letter
Art Bain
P.O. Box 602
Murray Hill Station
New York, NY 10156-0601
(212) 447-7328
Internet address:
corpletter@aol.com
$20 for four quarterly issues
Aimed at gay, lesbian, and bisexual employees, corporate human resource departments, and others concerned with gay issues in the workplace.

Working It Out
The Newsletter for Gay and Lesbian Employment Issues
Ed Mickens
P.O. Box 2079
New York, NY 10108
(212) 769-2384
Fax (212) 721-2680
$60 for four quarterly issues
Aimed at corporate human resource departments, management, and others concerned with gay issues in the workplace.

ORGANIZATIONS

WORKPLACE RELATED—LEGAL

These groups can provide information regarding domestic-partner benefits and discuss the laws that pertain to sexual orientation, AIDS, transgenderism, and other work-related issues.

American Civil Liberties Union (ACLU)
National Gay and Lesbian Rights Project
132 West 43rd Street
New York, NY 10036
(212) 944-9800 (ext. 545)

Gay and Lesbian Advocates and Defenders (GLAD)
P.O. Box 218
Boston, MA 02112
(617) 426-1350

Lambda Legal Defense and Education Fund
666 Broadway
12th floor
New York, NY 10012
(212) 995-8585

National Center for Lesbian Rights
1663 Mission Street
Suite 550
San Francisco, CA 94103
(415) 621-0674

National Lesbian and Gay Law Association
Box 77130
National Capital Station
Washington, DC 20014
(202) 389-0161

WORKPLACE RELATED—POLITICAL

These organizations coordinate national gay civil-rights efforts or are specifically devoted to work-related issues. They can provide information about what other corporations are doing, provide model non-discrimination policies, information on legislation, and other resources.

Hollywood Supports
6430 Sunset Boulevard
Suite 102
Los Angeles, CA 90028
(213) 962-3023

Human Rights Campaign Fund
1101 14th St. NW, Ste. 200
Washington, DC 20005
(202) 628-4160

Interfaith Center on Corporate Responsibility
475 Riverside Drive
Room 566
New York, NY 10115
(212) 870-2296

National Gay and Lesbian Task Force (NGLTF)
2320 17th St. NW
Washington, DC 20009-4309
(202) 332-6483

NGLTF Workplace Initiative
(415) 241-1565

Wall Street Project
    Community Lesbian and Gay Rights Institute
217 East 85th Street
Suite 162
New York, NY 10028
(212) 289-1741

EDUCATION

The following organizations can provide guidelines for curriculum development, suggest reading materials and appropriate audiovisuals, and offer continuing education opportunities and/or speakers.

American Association of Sex Educators, Counselors and
    Therapists (AASECT)
435 North Michigan Avenue
Suite 1717
Chicago, IL 60611-4067
(312) 644-0828

Campaign to End Homophobia
P.O. Box 819
Cambridge, MA 02139
(617) 868-8280

Center for Population Options
1025 Vermont Avenue, NW
Suite 210
Washington, DC 20005
(202) 347-5700

Parents and Friends of Lesbians and Gays (P-FLAG)
P.O. Box 27605
Washington, DC 20038-7605
(202) 638-4200

Planned Parenthood Federation of America
810 Seventh Avenue
New York, NY 10019
(212) 541-7800

Sex Information and Education Council of the United States
  (SIECUS)
130 West 42nd Street
Suite 2500
New York, NY 10036-7901
(212) 819-9770

AIDS INFORMATION

These organizations can provide accurate, up-to-date information about AIDS, suggest resources for AIDS education, provide or recommend trainers for workshops, and/or answer other AIDS-related questions.

AIDS Action Council
1875 Connecticut Avenue, NW
Suite 700
Washington, DC 20009
(202) 986-1300

American Foundation for AIDS Research (AmFAR)
733 Third Avenue
12th floor
New York, NY 10017
(212) 682-7440

The American Red Cross
1709 New York Avenue
Suite 208
Washington, DC 20006
(202) 662-1577

National AIDS Hotline
1-800-342-AIDS
1-800-344-SIDA (Spanish)
1-800-AIDS-TTY (Hearing Impaired)

National AIDS Information Clearinghouse
"Business Responds to AIDS"
Manager's Kit ($25)
P.O. Box 6003
Rockville, MD 20849-6003
1-800-458-5231

National Leadership Coalition on AIDS
1730 M Street, NW
Suite 905
Washington, DC 20036
(202) 429-0930

TRANSGENDER ISSUES

Human Outreach and Achievement Institute
405 Western Avenue
Suite 345
South Portland, ME 04106
(207) 621-0858

International Foundation for Gender Education
P.O. Box 367
Wayland, MA 01778
(617) 894-8340

Renaissance Education Association, Inc.
P.O. Box 60552
King of Prussia, PA 19406-0552
(215) 630-1437

BOOKS

GENERAL RESOURCE

These books direct the reader to valuable sources of information about the gay, lesbian, and bisexual communities.

The Big Gay Book
By John Preston
Plume, 1991

Gayellow Pages
Renaissance House
Box 292
Village Station
New York, NY 10014

GENERAL INFORMATION

These books provide a good overview of gay, lesbian, and bisexual people.

Another Mother Tongue: Gay Words, Gay Worlds
By Judy Grahn
Beacon Press, 1984

Bisexuality: A Reader and Sourcebook
Edited by T. Geller
Times Change Press, 1990

In Search of Gay America: Women and Men in a Time of Change
By Neil Miller
Atlantic Monthly Press, 1989

Looking at Gay and Lesbian Life
By Warren Blumenfeld and Diane Raymond
Philosophical Library, 1988

Making History: The Struggle for Gay and Lesbian Equal Rights
By Eric Marcus
HarperCollins, 1992

The New Loving Someone Gay
By Don Clark
Celestial Arts, 1992

On Being Gay: Thoughts on Family, Faith, and Love
By Brian McNaught
St. Martin's Press, 1988

Positively Gay
Edited by Betty Berzon
Celestial Arts, 1992

WORKPLACE RELATED

Coming Out of the Classroom Closet: Gay and Lesbian Students, Teachers and Curricula
Edited by Karen M. Harbeck
Harrington Park Press, 1992

The Corporate Closet: The Professional Lives of Gay Men in America
By James D. Woods and Jay H. Lucas
The Free Press, 1993

Cracking the Corporate Closet
By Dan Baker and Sean Strub
HarperCollins, 1993

Gays/Justice: A Study of Ethics, Society and Law
By Richard Mohr
Columbia University Press, 1988

Gay Workers: Trade Unions and the Law
By Chris Beer et al.
State Mutual Books, 1983

The 100 Best Companies for Gay Men and Lesbians
By Ed Mickens
Pocket Books, 1994

Our Diverse Work Force: A Survey of Issues and a Practical Guide
By Susan Carol Stone and Anthony Patrick Carnevale
U.S. Department of Labor and the American Society for Training and
Development, 1993

Pride at Work: Organizing for Lesbian and Gay Rights in Unions
By Miriam Frank and Desma Holcomb
Lesbian and Gay Labor Network
P.O. Box 1159-Peter Stuyvesant Station
New York, NY 10009

*The Rights of Lesbians and Gay Men: The Basic ACLU Guide to a Gay
Person's Rights*
By Nan Hunter, Sherryl Michaelson, and Thomas Stoddard
Southern University Press, 1992

HOMOPHOBIA

Homophobia: How We All Pay the Price
Edited by Warren Blumenfeld
Beacon Press, 1992

Homophobia: A Weapon of Sexism
By Suzanne Pharr
Chardon Press, 1988

Homophobia in American Society: Bashers, Baiters and Bigots
Edited by John P. DeCecco
Harrington Press, 1985

VIDEOS

WORKPLACE RELATED

*Gay Issues in the Workplace: Gay, Lesbian and Bisexual Employees Speak
for Themselves with Brian McNaught*, 1993

TRB Productions
P.O. Box 2362
Boston, MA 02107

GENERAL INFORMATION

The majority of these videos are available for purchase or rent from local gay and lesbian/feminist bookstores. For a listing of local bookstores, see the *Gayellow Pages*, cited above. If there is not a local source, contact Lambda Rising Bookstore, which is cited below. For a more thorough list of videos, contact the Campaign to End Homophobia.

Before Stonewall: The Making of the Gay and Lesbian Community, 1986

Common Threads: Stories from the Quilt, 1989

The Life and Times of Harvey Milk, 1986
Pacific Arts Video

On Being Gay: A Conversation with Brian McNaught, 1986
TRB Productions

Pink Triangles
Cambridge Documentary Films
Box 385
Cambridge, MA 02139
(617) 354-3677

Silent Pioneers: Gay and Lesbian Elders
Senior Action in a Gay Environment (SAGE)
Filmakers Library
124 East 40th Street
#901
New York, NY 10016
(212) 808-4980

Word Is Out: Stories of Some of Our Lives
New Yorker Films
16 West 61st Street
New York, NY 10023
(212) 247-6110

BROCHURES

NGLTF, the Campaign to End Homophobia, and P-FLAG have a variety of brochures that are useful educational tools. Listed here are a few of the most popular. Write for information on their other resources.

"Guide to Leading Introductory Workshops on Homophobia"
The Campaign to End Homophobia
P.O. Box 819
Cambridge, MA 02139
(617) 868-8280
Individuals $15, Organizations $25

"Homophobia"
The Campaign to End Homophobia
Individuals $5, Organizations $10

"Twenty Questions About Homosexuality"
NGLTF/Publications Department
2320 17th St. NW
Washington, DC 20009-4309
(202) 332-6483
$3

"Why Is My Child Gay?"
P-FLAG
P.O. Box 27605
Washington, DC 20038-7605
(202) 638-4200
$2

MATERIAL SOURCES

Lambda Rising Bookstore
Washington, DC
(800) 621-6969

21st Century News
1880 East River Road
Suite 210
Tucson, AZ 85718
(602) 577-1137
This company has a variety of educational videos available on gay,
lesbian, and bisexual issues.

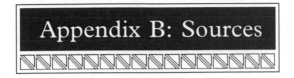

Appendix B: Sources

INTRODUCTION

1. Alfred C. Kinsey et al., *Sexual Behavior in the Human Male* and *Sexual Behavior in the Human Female* (Philadelphia and London: W. B. Saunders Co., 1948 and 1953). John O. G. Billy, Koray Tanfer, William R. Grady, and Daniel H. Klepinger, *Family Planning Perspectives* (Alan Guttmacher Institute, March/April 1993).

CHAPTER ONE

1. Kinsey et al., *Sexual Behavior in the Human Male* and *Female.*
2. Samuel S. Janus and Cynthia L. Janus, *The Janus Report on Sexual Behavior* (New York: John Wiley & Sons, 1993).
3. Billy et al., *Family Planning Perspectives.*
4. *WHO Press*, World Health Organization/United Nations (February 12, 1992).

CHAPTER THREE

1. Robert Crooks and Karla Baur, *Our Sexuality*, ed. Connie Spatz (New York: Benjamin Cummings Publishing Company, 1990). Gary Kelly, *Sexuality Today: The Human Perspective* (Guilford, Conn.: The Dushkin Publishing Group, 1990).
2. Crooks and Baur, *Our Sexuality.*
3. J. Michael Bailey, Ph.D. (Northwestern University Medical School), and Richard C. Pillard, M.D. (Boston University Medical School), *Archives of General Psychiatry* (December 1991 and March 1993).
4. Simon LeVay, Ph.D. (Salk Institute of Biological Studies), "A Difference in Hypothalamic Structure Between Heterosexual and Homosexual Men," *Science* (August 1991).
5. Laura Allen, M.D., and Roger Gorski, M.D. (UCLA School of Medicine), *Proceedings of the National Academy of Sciences* (August 1992).

6. Alan P. Bell, Martin S. Weinberg, and Sue Kiefer Hammersmith, *Sexual Preference: Its Development in Men and Women* (Bloomington: Indiana University Press, 1981).
7. C. S. Ford and F. A. Beach, *Patterns of Sexual Behavior* (New York: Harper and Bros., 1951).
8. Crooks and Baur, *Our Sexuality.*
9. Richard Plant, *The Pink Triangle: The Nazi War Against Homosexuals* (New York: Henry Holt & Co., 1988).

CHAPTER FOUR

1. Vivienne Cass, "Homosexual Identity Formation: A Theoretical Model," *Journal of Homosexuality*, vol. 4 (Spring 1979).

CHAPTER FIVE

1. Brian R. McNaught, "The Boston Project: Toward an Agenda for Gay and Lesbian Citizens," Executive Summary to Kevin H. White, Mayor of Boston (December 1983).
2. Gregory Herek, Ph.D., *Beyond "Homophobia": A Social Psychological Perspective on Attitudes Toward Lesbians and Gay Men* (Binghamton, N.Y.: The Haworth Press, 1984).
3. Gregory Herek, Ph.D., "Heterosexuals' Attitudes Toward Lesbians and Gay Men: Correlates and Gender Differences," *The Journal of Sex Research* (November 1988).

CHAPTER SIX

1. Art Bain, *Working It Out*, The Newsletter for Gay and Lesbian Employment Issues (Spring 1992).
2. Society for Human Resource Management, press release (March 9, 1993).
3. James M. Shannon, Attorney General, Commonwealth of Massachusetts, Personnel Manual, Department of the Attorney General (February 3, 1988).
4. David J. Jefferson, *Wall Street Journal* (May 18, 1992).
5. Russ Campanello, Vice President, Human Resources, Spousal Equivalent Benefits announcement to all U.S. Lotus employees (September 3, 1991).
6. David J. Barram, Vice President, Worldwide Corporate Affairs and Public Policies, letter to the Honorable Roy Romer, Governor of the State of Colorado (August 24, 1992).

CHAPTER SEVEN

1. *HIV/AIDS Surveillance*, Centers for Disease Control and Prevention (October 1992/January 14, 1993); *AIDS Newsletter*, Department of Public Health (January 1993); Dr. Jonathan Mann et al., *AIDS in the World*, Global AIDS Policy Coalition (1992).
2. Anthony Kosnik et al., *Human Sexuality: New Directions in American Catholic Thought*, a study commissioned by the Catholic Theological Society of America (New York: Paulist Press, 1977).
3. John Boswell, *Christianity, Social Tolerance, and Homosexuality: Gay People from the Beginning of the Christian Era to the Fourteenth Century* (Chicago: University of Chicago Press, 1980).
4. Judy Grahn, *Another Mother Tongue: Gay Words, Gay Worlds* (Boston: Beacon Press, 1984).
5. Crooks and Baur, *Our Sexuality*; Kelly, *Sexuality Today*.

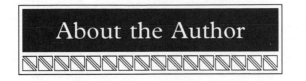

About the Author

BRIAN McNAUGHT IS an award-winning writer, sexuality educator, and consultant on the issues facing gay, lesbian, and bisexual people. In the last five years, he has trained several thousand employees of AT&T and Bell Communications Research (Bellcore) on the topic of "Homophobia in the Workplace." Since 1974, Mr. McNaught has spoken at nearly one hundred universities and has produced numerous educational materials on homosexuality and on Acquired Immune Deficiency Syndrome (AIDS). From 1982 to 1984 he served as the Mayor of Boston's liaison to the gay and lesbian community.

Mr. McNaught is the author of the popular book *On Being Gay: Thoughts on Family, Faith, and Love* (St. Martin's Press, 1988) and is featured in the videos "A Conversation with Brian McNaught on Being Gay" and "Gay Issues in the Workplace: Gay, Lesbian, and Bisexual Employees Speak for Themselves with Brian McNaught" (TRB Productions, 1986, 1993). He received his degree in journalism from Marquette University in 1970. A native of Detroit, Mr. McNaught now resides in Atlanta, Georgia.